Hayley
Westenra

Hayley Westenra

In her own voice

WITH DARREN HENLEY

First published in Great Britain in 2007 by
Virgin Books Ltd
Thames Wharf Studios
Rainville Road
London
W6 9HA

A catalogue record for this book is available from the British Library.

ISBN 978 1 9052 6420 9 (HB)
ISBN 978 0 7535 1366 8 (PB)

Penguin Random House is committed to a sustainable future for our business, our readers and our planet. This book is made from Forest Stewardship Council® certified paper.

MIX
Paper from
responsible sources
FSC® C018179

Typeset by TW Typesetting, Plymouth, Devon

Printed and bound in Great Britain by Clays Ltd, St Ives plc

Contents

Introduction

I am only twenty years old. It seems a very young age to be sitting down to write my autobiography. But so much has happened to me in the first two decades of my life that I wanted to commit it to paper before events start to merge together in my mind and become too hazy for me to remember them clearly.

For the very first time, I am telling my own story in my own voice. My life has been a truly remarkable journey so far. I have travelled the world, performing for kings and queens, princes and princesses, presidents and prime ministers.

I was lucky enough to be born with a voice that makes people stop and listen when I start to sing. It has not always been easy, though. There has been a lot of sweat – and there have been some tears – along the way. My parents have made enormous sacrifices to help me to live my dream.

Despite meeting all of these famous people around the world, I still love the things I have always loved: my sister Sophie; my brother Isaac; my bedroom in our house back in Christchurch; curling up on the sofa in my flat to watch *Coronation Street* on television in the evening; and eating rye bread smothered in Vegemite and mashed avocados.

I hope that becoming well known for my singing has not changed me one little bit. I do not think it has. In my mind, I am still little old Hayley from Christchurch in New Zealand. Once you have read my story, I hope that you will agree.

CHAPTER 1
KIWI AND PROUD OF IT

As I walked out through the players' tunnel on to the pitch of the Wales Millennium Stadium in Cardiff, I was hit by the scale of the place. Here was I, one small person with a microphone in her hand, standing in the centre of this enormous arena.

Wales has become my second home, so it seemed perfectly natural to me to be in Cardiff. I had become used to performing there alongside home-grown stars such as Bryn Terfel and Aled Jones. On this particular day, I was on the pitch with the soprano Katherine Jenkins. We were both to sing ahead of the Welsh rugby team's encounter with the mighty, all-conquering All Blacks.

You see, Wales may be my second home and I have been given the warmest of welcomes whenever I visit the 'Land of Song', but I will never forget my own home in Christchurch, New Zealand, thousands of miles away from Cardiff, right round the other side of the world. Wherever I go to perform, I always travel with my small Kiwi soft toy and a tiny New Zealand flag – both of which were given to me by a fan at one of my first big concerts. Now, it doesn't feel quite right if I haven't got them with me.

Since I first became the All Blacks' mascot and they chose me to sing the national anthem at the start of each of their matches, the guys have never lost a game. Not that they had much trouble on that front beforehand, to be honest. It has become a tight union between me and the team. I am thrilled to have the opportunity to support them and they like to have me there too. Not only do I get to sing, but I also have the bonus of getting free tickets to the game.

It is important for us Kiwis to stick together, since it can be easy to take the All Blacks' consistent success for granted. It was not until I travelled away from New Zealand that I realised just how magnificent and world-beating our rugby team actually is. Over the past few years, I have spent less time back home and more time travelling the world. This has made me even more patriotic. It has made me want to grab hold of anything that reminds me of home and hold it close. So, whenever I have the opportunity to sing the national anthem, which tends to be at rugby matches, I sing it with such passion. That connection to my country means so much to me; it fills me with such pride.

Standing in the middle of the Millennium Stadium pitch, I could feel my emotions brimming over. I was really enjoying the sense of anticipation, energy and excitement that was radiating from the crowd. Despite the fact that millions of people were watching around the world on television, and tens of thousands of people were surrounding me in the stadium, strangely enough, I did not feel even the slightest twinge of nerves.

After Katherine and I had walked out on to the pitch with the teams, all eyes and ears were on us as we each sang our country's anthems. That afternoon, it was as if I were discovering the power of 'God Defend New Zealand' for the first time. I was able to ride on the positive waves of energy of the crowd, and I guess this is why I was so nerveless. I knew that everyone had come to see a great game of rugby, and so the attention was not really on me. The people who were feeling the pressure were the players. My job was to lend my team as much support as possible.

Having such a strong and successful rugby team playing for your country definitely does help. I know that we Kiwis should never become arrogant, but winning so often and so convincingly always makes me feel just a little more confident, when I am singing alongside the guys. Maybe if I was singing for another team, then I might not be quite so sure of myself.

Singing the New Zealand anthem that afternoon was almost like an out-of-body experience. I was standing on the pitch with my microphone, but it felt as if I were one of the Kiwi supporters in the crowd, some of whom had spent 24 hours in a plane just to be there that afternoon. I love singing the anthem *a cappella* because I can fall in with the crowd's tempo. After all, there are more of them than there is of me and, even though I have the microphone and the loud speakers on my side, they can still make more noise. If I sing to a backing track, I can sometimes feel that I am not singing with the crowd because they are slightly out of time.

This particular afternoon, though, it was perfect. The noise was so loud that I struggled to hear myself sing at all – but that is all part of the buzz of performing the anthem.

5

When it came to a close, the crowd let out a huge roar of approval.

The other great tradition at the start of an All Blacks game is the *haka*, the traditional Maori war dance, where the team ask the gods to give them strength. It is a fantastically powerful sight and sound and it never fails to bring a lump to my throat. On this occasion, they performed it in their dressing room and it was beamed around the stadium on big screens before the players came out.

Katherine and I walked off the pitch with the cheers ringing in our ears. I had learned from bitter experience that the one thing that you should never wear on a rugby pitch is stiletto heels because you sink into the grass. For me, the nightmare scenario would be having to ask two burly players to lift me out of the ground after becoming welded to the pitch. Although she had performed the Welsh national anthem many, many times on the pitch before, I remember Katherine had a slight wardrobe malfunction and had forgotten to wear suitable footwear for the long walk to and from the anthem singers' podium. She was far more relieved finally to get off the pitch than I was. Although, I must say that they were very nice shoes.

As much as I love Wales and the people who live there, when it comes to rugby, they will only ever be my number-two team, so I was delighted when the All Blacks triumphed in the game.

I have sung with Katherine at the Millennium Stadium on many occasions, including once when it had been decided just 24 hours before the game that I should duet with her on the Welsh national anthem. That meant that I had less than a day to learn the words. They were, of course, in Welsh. Not the easiest of languages to master quickly, but I managed to get myself just about word perfect in time for the kick-off, after spending half the night listening to it over and over again on my iPod.

On one occasion I somehow found myself travelling back to the All Blacks' hotel in the team bus. Kathryn Nash, who is one of my managers, was with me at the time and we could not quite get over how lucky we were to have this privilege – and a police escort, too! We realised very quickly that it was quite a testosterone-filled vehicle and it was initially just a little bit intimidating. But they were all perfect gentlemen and I loved every minute of the trip – especially the serenade. Yes, you heard me right. I was serenaded by the All Blacks the whole way back to their hotel. The All Blacks players are incredibly down to earth, nowhere near the ego-driven self-regarding superstars that you might find in some other sports. As I watched them relaxing after the game, I had to remind myself quite how much pressure is placed on their shoulders. True, they do get an enormous amount of praise to balance out that pressure. But, the moment there is even the slightest suggestion of a crack in their invincibility, the temperature really hots up for them.

It got me thinking. Although it may seem very different at first sight, there are quite a few similarities between playing rugby and being a singer as a career. In both jobs, to get to the top you need to follow a strict training regime, respecting and looking after your body at all times. If you become sick or unfit, then your performance can be seriously impaired. That one word – performance – is really important. A rugby player goes on to the pitch to give the performance of his life for each of the forty-minute halves of the match. A singer goes on to the stage to give the performance of her life for each of the forty-minute halves of the concert. The players have to be disciplined to achieve that and that is why I can relate to them so well. It is the discipline that we have in common.

When we arrived back at the team hotel, I did feel a little awkward getting off the bus with all the guys, as their fans gathered around the bus patiently waiting for autographs. I hoped that they did not feel that I was some sort of interloper.

The All Blacks' after-match parties always have a great atmosphere. Everyone is really chilled. They are a very close bunch with an outstanding team spirit and camaraderie, led by Richie McCaw, our current captain. In order to play as they do on the pitch, I think they have to have this very special bond. It must be one of the reasons why they are such a great team: they are all so close. When they are on tour, they play together and live together and work together. They look out for each other as well. One of the nicest things for me about hanging out with them is that I get the sense that they are looking out for me as well. They treat me like one of the team.

I don't want to single out any of the players, because you can't have favourites when they are your family. But I do love Piri Weepu because not only is he an incredible player, but he is also an incredible singer and dancer, which earns him extra brownie points in my book! He is usually at the front of the action when it comes to starting the singalong in the team room during the evening. The players have an enormous repertoire of New Zealand 'guy songs' by artists such as Dave Dobbyn and Bob Marley. They are the sorts of songs that I recognise from hearing guys singing back home, but as they would never normally be sung by a girl I hadn't bothered committing them to memory.

As the after-match party continued and each of the players performed his party piece, I could foresee the inevitability that I would have to sing. This was not time or the place for the delicate beauty of 'Pie Jesu' or 'Ave Maria', so I began silently to hope that they would all be too tired to continue before it was my turn. In the meantime, I was racking my brain for something suitable.

'Come on, Hayley! It's your turn!' came the cry suddenly from one of the players in the corner.

'Do you know any Stevie Wonder songs?' I asked the guitarist hopefully.

'What about "Lately"?' came the reply.

I just about knew all the words, so I led the team in a stirring rendition of 'Lately'. It was great. Here was I, sitting in a hotel, jamming with the All Blacks. Now, there are not many people in the world who can say that they've done that.

CHAPTER 2
THE PLACE I CALL HOME

Life is pretty laid back in New Zealand. It is very cut off from the rest of the world, so a lot of the country is quite untouched, especially down in the South Island, which is where I come from. The views are breathtaking and the landscape is stunningly beautiful and largely unspoiled by development. Christchurch, where I was born, has a population of around half a million people. We have a cathedral and that makes us a city, but, as cities go, we are definitely on the small side.

When I was starting out on my singing career, Christchurch was plenty big enough for me. Eventually, though, there was a point when I realised that I would have to go up to Auckland, the big smoke in New Zealand, and then ultimately overseas to fulfil my dreams. But, for the first decade or so of my life, Christchurch was my world.

Although Christchurch has always been home for me, my family on neither my mum's side nor my dad's side originate there. The way in which my mum, Jill, met my dad, Gerald, has always seemed very bizarre to me.

Now, I love him very much, but I have to be honest and say that Dad really is not the most musical man on earth. Mum used to do a bit of singing, but it was Dad rather than she who had somehow got himself a singing role in a musical production of *Bugsy Malone*. Mum had just arrived in Christchurch from Timaru and they met at the after-show party. The rest, as they say, is history and they have been together ever since.

Westenra is actually a Dutch name and my family on Dad's side emigrated from Holland to Ireland and then on to New Zealand. Dad's mother, Patricia, died when I was just three years old, so I do not remember her now. Sadly, I also never met my paternal grandfather, Aylmer, who died when Dad was fourteen. In the stories that Dad has told me, he always sounds like a heroic kind of guy. He contracted polio when he was working out in Kenya and so was confined to a wheelchair. His disability never affected his sharp mind, though, and he was forever thinking up new inventions, including a night-and-day globe, which was sadly never put into production before he died.

Mum's maiden name is actually Ireland. Her parents, Shirley and Gerry, were second-generation Kiwis. They owned a bed-and-breakfast on the West Coast and Grandad also drove the delivery lorries for the local brewery.

My grandmother, Shirley Ireland, is still a very important person in my life. She used to be a great singer, but sadly her voice was affected by the radiotherapy that was used to treat breast cancer. Grandad was incredibly musical, playing the piano accordion, the piano, the harmonica (in all of its different sizes) and the violin. Together with Nanna, he would travel around the hotels and pubs near their home putting on entertainment. She would sing the hits of the time – the sort of music made famous by Vera Lynn during and after World War Two – and he would accompany her.

During their childhood, Mum and her sister, my Auntie Carol, were regularly taken out for drives in the car by Grandad and Nanna on Sunday lunchtimes. Invariably, they would end up at a local pub and the two girls would run about in the adjoining playground, once they had been bought a treat such as a raspberry drink or a Crunchie bar. Grandad always had his piano accordion in the boot of his car, just in case the opportunity arose to bring it out. The opportunity nearly always did arise. So Nanna would sing and Mum and Auntie Carol would join in with their own version of the Highland fling.

Eventually, the four of them moved to Timaru on the east coast, where Mum went to high school. For as long as I can remember, we have always gone down to Timaru for Easter and Christmas. When we were small, the house was always filled with sound: lots of music and lots of singing. My brother, sister and I would regularly put on a show for our grandparents. It was always a big deal and the three of us used to practise in my room, working on harmonies. The music that they brought into our lives made them one of my earliest and most important musical influences.

When I was as young as three years old, I can remember sitting on Grandad's lap as he played the piano accordion. When he played the piano, I would jump up and perform my latest ballet moves alongside him. His talent was all the more remarkable, since he would play all these instruments by ear, never having had any formal lessons. I loved the way his fingers would run up and down the piano keyboard. He played with such ease. I really don't know how he did it.

Mum and Dad are polar opposites – very much yin and yang. Mum is constantly on the go. It always seems to me that, even when she should be taking it easy, she is still flying around at rocket speed. There's always something which needs to be done urgently, so she is permanently busy and bustling. There is the odd occasion where she will sit down at the dining room table for a moment with a cup of coffee and a couple of squares of chocolate, while she reads a newspaper or magazine. But then, after just a few minutes, she will be out of the door again, racing off to pick something up or to see someone.

Right now, while I am writing this book, it is the renovation of our house that is occupying a considerable amount of Mum's time. She puts a lot of thought into all of her projects and, at the moment, every conversation I have with her includes a good proportion of house talk. Mum invests so much effort in things. She will never go into a shop and make a snap decision over buying, say, a skirt. She will always ask, 'Will it work with this top? Does it go with these shoes?'

Dad, on the other hand, is very laid back. To be honest, I don't think they would still be together if either Mum were as laid back as he is, or Dad were on the go as much as Mum. She is the worrier, but he is very chilled. Me? I think I'm lucky enough to be a mixture of the best bits of the two of them!

When they first got together, Dad was a surfer dude and Mum says he was eating terribly, with his diet consisting of virtually nothing other than milk shakes. She was always very interested in natural medicine and health, so she taught him about the benefits of healthy eating. He took the advice to heart and nowadays he is the one sticking to the healthy-eating regime fairly religiously, which Mum finds just a tad frustrating, as she succumbs to yet another chocolate craving. I am on Mum's side for this one. I think it's a woman thing!

After they were married, Dad took a job in a jewellery shop and worked his way up to being the manager. He decided to study gemmology, as he figured it would be a little more stimulating than simply climbing the business ladder. He learned a range of skills, including identifying precious stones and grading diamonds for insurance policies. These skills were put in practice when he opened his jewellery-valuation business around thirteen years ago.

Mum was training to be a teacher when she became pregnant with me. This was a great opportunity for her to put all of her interest in healthy eating and naturopathy into practice. She did all of her research on what food to eat to increase the probability of having a healthy baby, becoming something of an expert on the subject in the process. She really is one of those people who, if they are going to do something, do it properly, whatever it is.

I was born on 10 April 1987 and named Hayley Dee Westenra. My parents felt that Hayley Dee had a nice ring to it. Hayley was chosen because Mum and Dad were fans of the actress Hayley Mills. I was a very contented child and am told that I was very undemanding.

My sister, Sophie Larelle Westenra, came along three years after. Our little brother, Isaac Ireland Westenra, was born three years after Sophie. His unusual middle name was in tribute to Mum's maiden name.

I love my brother and sister very much; they are both wonderful people. I find it hard to believe that Sophie is seventeen and is already in her final year of high school. It is quite scary really, because in my mind she is still 'little Sophie', still very vulnerable and very small, which is really not the case at all any more.

Sophie is lucky to be both musical and intellectual. I'm very proud that she's always been near the top in nearly all of her classes. At the same time, she has a brilliant singing voice. Her biggest dilemma is deciding which direction to take in terms of a future career. Either way, I know she is going to make her mark on the world, so watch this space.

Isaac, who is fourteen, is very much a cross between Mum and Dad. Because there are six years between us, we have never fought or squabbled. I was very much his 'big sister'. He's very laid back, but at the same time he's a real detail person. Growing up, he was always very interested in inventing things. He liked to draw intricate little diagrams of his inventions and then talk me through them in great detail.

Isaac was quite a shy kid, but he's recently come right out of his shell. Growing up, he's always had a beautiful voice. He would join in with Sophie and me, but he was always quite a reluctant performer. When I was last at home, he spent the whole time singing and playing his guitar. I was left in awe of my little brother's newfound skill and pizzazz. He has become a great rock performer and gives some brilliant renditions of the hits of bands such as Nickelback and the Red Hot Chili Peppers.

Christchurch was a great place to grow up. These days it would not be ideal for me to live there because it's so far away from the other countries where I perform most often. But, when I was a youngster, it had everything I could possibly want, and living there gave me the chance to have a really wholesome upbringing.

The weather in that part of New Zealand is very mild. The winters are never too harsh and the summers are never too hot, making it a very enjoyable climate. Even in the depths of winter, I used to get up early and run outside. I loved the sound of the frost scrunching under foot. Although the air was very crisp, the sun was nearly always still shining. When

I was very small, Mum would often take me out to feed the ducks in the local park, which was just a short walk down the road.

One of the many benefits of living in New Zealand is that Kiwis tend to lead a very outdoor sort of life. Children have a very free lifestyle and it's quite normal to have a playhouse or tree house in your backyard.

New Zealand is a big enough place with a small enough number of inhabitants to mean that most people are lucky enough to be able to have a decent patch of land to call their own. Our backyard was big enough for us to run around in to our hearts' content. We still had space for a trampoline and a playhouse, as well as jungle bars (a sort of metal climbing frame). We built tree huts at the end of the garden and we happily spent hours clambering in and out of them, creating imaginary worlds as we went. Behind our house, we had yet another hut – this one built among the firewood. There were holes in the fences between our garden and those of our neighbours each side, meaning that all the children could run between the houses without ever having to venture outside the safety of our backyards.

Underneath my bedroom window, I had my own little area of garden, which I would lovingly tend. In our vegetable garden, we planted parsley, garden peas, silver beets and lettuce – all the 'easy-to-grow' vegetables.

I desperately wanted a pet and plagued Mum and Dad. It turned out that our record of animal ownership was not a fantastic success to begin with. First, we had a cat called Tammy, but Sophie proved to be allergic to cats, so poor old Tammy was shipped off to live with Auntie Carol.

I was besotted with rabbits when I was small and had a collection of soft toy bunnies. Perhaps it's because I was born in the Chinese Year of the Rabbit that I've such affinity to them. The decision was taken that I would be given a pet rabbit for my eighth birthday. Being a little sister, Sophie wanted everything that I had when we were kids, so she had a rabbit too. At just five years old, she was too small to look after hers, so the rabbit-care duties fell to me. We were never keen on keeping them locked up in their cage all day every day, so we had Dad build some special rabbit runs, putting his famous Kiwi ingenuity to use. I always ended up in charge of keeping an eye on the rabbits, Peter and Snowdrop, as they pottered about their grassy patch. On one occasion, when I didn't have my eye on them, they escaped, much to my horror. We managed to catch them, but after that scare Dad blocked off all the rabbit-sized escape routes from the back garden. We gave up on the runs and instead let the rabbits run free around the yard when we were out with them. But our rabbits just kept on growing and the bigger they became, the faster they seemed to be able to run away from us.

We had the best of intentions because we didn't want to keep them cooped up in a cage, but, every time we let them run free, we then had to spend hours running after them trying to put them back into the safety of their cage for the night time.

Eventually we gave both of the rabbits away, and mine, Snowdrop, was last heard of eating the cabbages and flowers in the gardens neighbouring her new home.

Our quest to find a suitable pet was not yet over, though. We opted for something a little smaller and so bought two mice – one for me and one for Sophie. My mouse, who went by the name of Snoopy, developed a scab on its back, so we used to have to put ointment on it every day.

In the end, the mice were handed on to new homes as well. After we'd tried a cat, rabbits and mice, you might have thought that we would have given up on pet ownership altogether – but then we alighted on our perfect pet, who arrived on my eleventh birthday. Zac, the cockatiel, still lives with the family today. He is a small grey bird and he can talk a little, although I think he might be envious that he cannot sing. At least, whenever I sing and he's nearby, he makes a terrible racket. It's possible he might be trying to join in, but, equally, he could be voicing his disapproval.

We thought it was very normal at the time, but looking back I realise now that we enjoyed a very creative childhood. Mum definitely encouraged it, putting into practice what she had learned when she trained to be a teacher. She knew all about child development and I'm sure it was no accident that, in the corner of our house, we had a box filled with all sorts of arts-and-crafts materials so that we could make anything that our imaginations could come up with. Next to it was another box full of different outfits and clothes for us to dress up in. These were things that I took for granted as a child. The one thing we definitely didn't do was to sit in front of the television during all our spare time.

I always had a fascination with making things. In one way, I was a bit of a tomboy. Although I loved fairies and was utterly convinced that a group of them lived at the end of our garden, I definitely didn't like Barbie dolls. I loved using sticking tape, scissors and glue to create random bits and pieces that, back then, I thought needed to be created. I was a big fan of modelling clay and it was always top of my list of Christmas-present requests. When I get time even now, I still make some of my own jewellery. Whenever we went to the beach, I would pick up the shiniest or most interesting-looking shells and stones and would keep them in little collections in my bedroom.

Once, I even dug out a pond in our backyard. I used my toy spade to dig a hole, before lining it with a plastic sheet. I placed dirt around the top of the plastic to keep it in place and to hide it from view. Then I filled it with water. There were one or two design faults in my little pond and, very quickly, it ended up as a big pool of mud. But that didn't matter, because it was my pond. Mum and Dad had given me the freedom to make it all by myself.

One of my favourite movies as a child was *The Secret Garden*. As soon as I watched it, I knew that I just had to have a secret garden all of my own. One of my friends helped me to cut a hole in a bush below my bedroom window among the shrubs. That allowed me to get into a tiny clearing about the size of a doormat that would become my secret garden. Or, at least, that was what we set out to do. Instead, we ended up hacking off half the bush, killing it in the process. I was in big trouble! I'm not sure that Mum has ever quite forgiven me. So, although we were given the freedom to be creative, there were definitely parameters. We knew where the line was and we knew when we had crossed it.

Some of my favourite memories of my entire childhood are of being in the backyard at home. Whether we were up in the tree house, hiding in the playhouse, climbing through the fence to next door, jumping on the trampoline or splashing around in the paddling pool, it was just a great existence. And I will always be indebted to Mum and Dad for that.

CHAPTER 3
THE LITTLEST STAR IS BORN

When I was growing up, I was constantly surrounded by music. Mum would play classical music to me when I was a baby, because she had read the research suggesting that listening to classical music can help a very young child's brain development. Later, as a youngster, due to my troubled sleeping, Mum and Dad bought me a collection of classical-music tapes to play in the background as a way of gently lulling me to sleep each night.

Those tapes were filled with classical favourites, such as Mozart's *Eine Kleine Nachtmusik* and Tchaikovsky's ballets *Nutcracker* and *Swan Lake*.

I can't remember my earliest performance, but I'm told that it happened when I was a flower girl at Auntie Carol's wedding. I was still a toddler, but apparently I sang a nonstop stream of Christmas carols right the way through the service. Singing to myself became more and more of a habit, but my parents didn't pick up on my voice as being in any way special. They just assumed that all kids sang the way I did.

When I was five years old, I went to Fendalton Primary School. To be honest with you, Fendalton is quite a posh area and our house's location made us borderline cases to be allowed to go there. Mum was never a typical Fendalton parent. There were a lot of students from very wealthy homes there and Mum was probably the only parent among them who would regularly go off to other school fairs to buy cheap clothes. She planned these buying trips with military precision, getting up at the crack of dawn and then arriving back home a few hours later with plastic bags full of clothes for each of us. During our childhoods, most of our clothes were second-hand because, although we were not what you would class as needy, there was never loads of cash to go around. That meant that Mum and Dad needed to budget very carefully. Without doubt, I've inherited that thriftiness and I'm still very conscious of not wasting money today.

Fendalton Primary was a lovely school at which to be a student. I was quite shy as a child, but it was my classroom teacher when I was six years old, Lesley Compton, who noticed that I could sing. It goes to show what a good teacher she was, because, even though I didn't say much, she still homed in on the fact that this was the thing that I was good at, even though there were around thirty other children vying for her attention every day. She gave me the solo in the Christmas school play, singing 'The Littlest Star'.

Now, not only was I shy at school, but I didn't say that much at home at the time either. I've certainly made up for that since, but back then I was not the greatest communicator.

'I need to take my ballet gear to school today,' I told Mum on the morning of the big performance.

'Here you go,' she replied. Mum and Dad turned up to watch the school play that afternoon, as all conscientious parents would do. They sat down and got a huge shock when they opened up their programmes to read 'The Littlest Star – Hayley Westenra'.

I really didn't understand that it was in any way a big deal. I was very calm about the performance and was not even the slightest bit worried. At that age, you tend not to realise that performing in public could possibly be frightening. I went on stage and sang my song faultlessly. The audience applauded very warmly and I beamed out from the stage at Mum and Dad. I couldn't understand why they seemed to have tears in their eyes.

At the end of the concert, Mrs Compton approached Mum and Dad and commented on my musical nature, suggesting that I should start learning a musical instrument. We went through the options. I didn't like the idea of learning something brassy and loud such as the trumpet one little bit, so in the end we settled on the violin, which makes a wonderfully melodic sound, a little like singing.

Music really became my thing at primary school and, although I was still shy, I was very driven in a quiet and understated sort of way. Even my family were sometimes quite surprised when I exhibited signs of steely determination. I do remember becoming frustrated that I suffered a little from 'tall-poppy syndrome' at school, where, as soon as one pupil started to shine at something, he or she would be cut back down. I struggled to understand why I was sometimes not chosen for singing roles, when I knew, based on a rational judgement, that I had a better voice than those who *were* picked. When I look back on it now, I realise that I was frighteningly focused for someone who was still so small. I also noticed that the one exception to the 'tall-poppy syndrome' was sport. If you excelled at sport, that seemed to be nurtured to a greater extent.

I was never great at sport, but I always gave it a go. I played netball for a while. I was always the shortest in my class, so it was not the best option. On the athletics field, I hated the high jump and was terrified of this bar looming towards me as I ran up and took off.

For a short period, I tried karate because it was something that Dad and Sophie were keen on doing, but it was much more their kind of thing than mine. Dad was keen that we learn it for self-defence. Sophie was far more determined to work her way through the belts ahead of me. Being the younger sister, she's quite competitive with me in that respect. She was delighted when she became a yellow belt before I did.

If I had a sporting forte, it was on the cross-country running course. This is quite a solitary individual sport and it fitted my personality far better than a team game. Even now, I'm far happier working as a soloist than in an ensemble. There are good and bad points about being part of a group, but I feel that, if you work in a group situation, you can sometimes be swayed in the wrong direction by the views of others in the group. I much prefer having my own space; I like to be in control of my life and to be able to plan my days around what I want to do. Mum always gives me a hard time about it, saying, 'What happens when you meet a guy? Eventually, you'll have to compromise.' I'm sure that I will in the end. It's not that I'm stuck in my ways, but I do like to be in charge of my own life.

When I was at Fendalton Primary, I did quite well on my natural ability, as opposed to having to put in lots of hard work. My school reports often commented on my inability to hand in my homework on time. It was a constant theme and my problem was twofold. True, I would procrastinate a little, but I was also a perfectionist and I always wanted to get everything right. Some kids would rush their homework, saying, 'I don't really care, as long as it's done.' But I was the opposite. I never wanted to hand something in to the teacher that was not done to the best of my ability. I'm still that way today and I always want everything I do to be spot on. I hate the thought that I had the opportunity to do something better and I didn't take it.

When I was seven years old, a family friend told Mum about some local auditions for *The Sound of Music*. She thought that I might be interested. Up until then, it had never occurred to me to develop an interest in musicals, but it seemed like a good idea. So, I went along to audition for the part of Marta. I remember hearing all of the other kids singing and knowing that I was better than they were. This might read as my being arrogant or big-headed, but I promise you that this was not the case. I was still a quiet, thoughtful child and I came to this conclusion in a very rational way rather than through arrogance. As I stood there at the auditions, I gradually began to realise that I was not only a good singer when I compared myself with the other children in my school, but I was actually doing pretty well when compared with the talent in the rest of Christchurch.

It was at that point that I really grasped the idea that singing was 'my thing'. It made me even more focused and excited that I had discovered my calling. It gave me a sense of direction and I thought, Right, this is it – singing. I want to be a singer.

Alongside the singing, I developed an interest in dancing and acting. My ballet teacher, when I was around the age of eight, was very encouraging. She told me that I had the perfect physique for a dancer: my body shape was right and I was good at the moves. But I was getting busier and busier, so in the end the dancing had to come second to the singing. There was a danger that I would be spreading myself too thinly. At one stage, later in my career, I had ambitions to be an all-round entertainer, a singer who branched into acting. But these days, that does not appeal at all. I'm more than happy to stick with my singing and my songwriting. Maybe in time I'll not only be singing and writing, but arranging too – which I have actually already started doing – as well as producing my albums. All these fields can work hand in hand, but I do think it's really important to stick to what you're good at, so I'll see how I go. Dancing is something that I would love to get back into as a hobby, but I obviously realise that I'm never going to be a professional. It's a great form of expression, though.

I continued learning the violin and doing ballet right through until I was about fourteen. I did all the exams, but my singing started to get in the way, especially of the ballet. I had reached Grade Six and my teacher said, 'Just come to a couple of lessons a week.' But I felt that I was getting behind the class, so I decided, reluctantly, to give it up. The lessons were starting to seem like a hassle, especially when it was cold and we all had to stand there in our leotards learning how to *plié* (a knee-bending movement) correctly for hours on end.

My extracurricular activities sometimes caused a problem at school. Rather than going down the more conservative route of doing singing lessons and taking structured exams, I was taking part in musicals and working on the fringes of professional theatre. Because of that, I would miss the odd class or take a day off school if I had been up late the previous night. And the teachers didn't always approve of my doing that sort of thing.

After I had cut my teeth on stage singing 'The Littlest Star', if I was offered any opportunity whatsoever to sing or perform, I would take it. Talent Quest competitions are popular across New Zealand and it was probably inevitable that someone as keen on performing as I was would end up becoming a regular competitor.

These competitions, which usually happen in shopping malls, are open to anyone: singers, dancers and musicians. You name it, they were there. As well as some fantastic talents, there were also those people who just wanted to get up on stage and have a go. Nobody minded if it was a dance that they had put together in their bedroom to Britney Spears's 'Hit Me Baby One More Time'. The important thing was that they were going for it.

I entered these competitions with gusto. I loved the challenge of working my way through the heats and trying to reach the finals. It was a great opportunity to get out there and perform – and perhaps to show off a bit as well. One of my biggest tasks surrounding Talent Questing was to find backing music for the songs. My repertoire included 'Walking in the Air' from *The Snowman*, the Celine Dion track 'Because You Loved Me', Andrew Lloyd Webber's 'Unexpected Song' and 'Time to Say Goodbye', which was made famous by Andrea Bocelli and Sarah Brightman.

I took the competitions very seriously, although I probably didn't practise as much as some of the contestants did. In particular, the dancers must have had to put in an amazing amount of hard work to perfect their routines. Things were going well at various Talent Quests, but one day it all went wrong in a contest at the South City shopping mall.

I was singing 'Because You Love Me' and I walked on stage as normal, but I didn't hear the music starting, so I missed my cue. This threw me completely and I was not experienced enough to know how to recover. I panicked and my voice went off key for the rest of the performance. In truth, it was probably the wrong song for me to sing in the first place. The judges didn't like the performance one little bit and I failed to make it through to the finals.

It was a good lesson for me because, up until that point, I had always expected to succeed. I was in floods of tears on the way home. It was my biggest performing failure and I felt so embarrassed. I vowed to myself that I was never going to sing ever again in the whole world. Despite everyone's best efforts, I was inconsolable.

When we arrived home, I ran into my bedroom and hid between the side of my bed and my bedroom window, so that nobody could see me. Mum came and sat on my bed and tried to talk it through with me.

'I don't want to talk about it!' I wailed. When things go wrong, I much prefer to shut myself off and come to terms with things on my own. As I look back on it now, it seems unthinkable that I would have even considered giving up singing, but at the time it was the end of the world.

'I'm so embarrassed I messed up in front of all those people,' I sobbed to Mum. 'My reputation's ruined.'

'Well, look,' she consoled me. 'You can give up if you want to. Or you can learn from it and keep carrying on.'

Eventually, I came to my senses and used the whole experience as part of the learning curve that is necessary for any live performer. After that, we all used to sit down around the kitchen table following each of the Talent Quests to talk through what went right and what went wrong on each particular occasion.

By now, Sophie was also involved in the Talent Quests as well, so they turned into a major family affair. The discussions in the car on the way home and over dinner around the kitchen table became longer and more detailed. We became experts on the judges' likes and dislikes and developed a keen eye for analysing our competitors' strengths and weaknesses too.

My greatest Talent Quest triumph came at the Northlands Mall, near to my home. I was eleven years old and sang 'The Mists of Islay', a very beautiful and haunting folk song. It was an unusual choice for that sort of environment, where the latest pop hits are far more the order of the day. I guess I stood out because of that. I worked my way through the heats and into the final of the junior section, which I was delighted to win. Then I had to go up against the winner of the senior section to see which of us would be named overall champion. I couldn't believe it when the senior judge read out my name. Not only did I win NZ$1,750 for myself, I also earned my school a cheque for NZ$1,000.

After I had performed, one of the judges went out and bought me a Kathleen Battle CD.

'I think you could sound like her if you keep going in the direction you're going in,' she told me as she handed over her gift.

These days, I'm singing a lot of classical music, but back then my singing style was similar to that of any young girl. My voice was very natural and not at all classical, but, then again, by choosing a song such as 'The Mists of Islay', I was not positioning myself as a pop artist either. When I listened to the Kathleen Battle CD, I was very taken with her voice. She has a very pure, clean sound and her voice is extremely agile. I was very touched by the compliment that the lady had paid to me.

The victory at Northlands Mall came just after I had completed my time at Fendalton Primary School and just before I was due to join Cobham Intermediate School. It meant that I was able to arrive at my new school with a cheque for a cool NZ$1,000.

'Well, you know, we feel really bad about accepting this, because we haven't really done anything for it yet,' said my lovely principal, Trevor Beaton.

'Don't worry, you will!' replied Mum with a smile.

And she was right. I had a wonderful two years at the school. It was another very supportive place to learn. The teachers very quickly hooked into my love of music and I was given the lead role in the school play, *Alice in Wonderland*. I was so excited, not just because I had the opportunity to sing and act, but because I was actually playing the title part. Just recently, I visited the school again to open their new music suite, which I'm very honoured to have named after me.

I remained quietly competitive as each of the Talent Quest competitions came along. I had been given a taste of winning and I really rather liked it.

'You come across as so nice and sweet,' Mum told me one day. 'But people don't realise that you're really tough.'

I don't think she meant 'tough' in a horrible way, but I was very focused and quietly determined to work my way up.

Child stars are always asked, 'Were your parents pushy?' I can honestly reply that my parents never pushed me in any direction that I didn't already want to go in. Dad always tended to take a back seat in these things; Mum would always encourage us to practise our instruments and our singing, but she would never push us into doing it.

I know that I would never have achieved everything that I've done today without my wonderful Mum. I knew from a very early age that I wanted to go on stage and that I wanted to be involved in musicals.

About this time, she said to me, 'Hayley, you've just started intermediate school. You shouldn't be doing any more musicals. You should be concentrating on your schoolwork.'

'Oh, I guess you're right,' I would grudgingly reply. But then I would hear about another set of auditions and 'Mum, can I just try out?' would come the plaintive request.

Inevitably, I would then win the part. Mum always supported us wholeheartedly in anything we chose to do, and, once we had decided on something, she would make it happen to the best of her ability. For example, she used to spend hours helping me to sort out the backing music for the Talent Quests. Nowadays, it's a lot easier to locate music with the Internet being more advanced, but back then it was really tough. It was a struggle for all the singers in the competitions to get hold of good arrangements. Some kids would even resort to singing along to the original recording complete with the original vocals – something that just didn't work at all. These were the kids who were not lucky enough to have parents who spent time helping them, so, to my mind, it does pay to have a mum and a dad who want to be involved.

But I think that, if they had pushed me, I would have probably resented it. If singing was not something that I had wanted to do, and they had forced me into it, I would have given up long before now.

CHAPTER 4
LEARNING MY CRAFT

On a sunny weekend, you will generally find a couple of buskers performing in the Arts Centre area of Christchurch. A few others are usually milling around, awaiting their turn. I ended up becoming a busker by accident. It all began after I had joined the Canterbury Opera Children's Chorus, which is now known as Canterbury Opera Youth. A group of us were putting on a concert as part of the Festival of Romance at the Arts Centre.

We had a lunch break after a busy morning of rehearsals, but a few of us didn't have any money with us to buy food.

One of the gang pointed to a busker down the street and suggested that we go outside and try our luck as buskers to see if we could earn some cash. So, more as a joke than anything else, five or six of us went out on the street and sang some of the songs we had spent the morning rehearsing – songs from operas and operettas – quite high-end classical stuff.

It went surprisingly well and, after we had given our performance with the Canterbury Opera Children's Chorus, one of the guys from the group turned to me and said, 'How about we do some more busking?'

So we sang all of the songs we knew and things went very well on the money front. When Mum and Sophie came to pick me up, Sophie joined in and we ended up splitting the afternoon's takings three ways. We had each made enough to buy not just lunch that day, but for the next couple of weeks, had we wanted to.

When I arrived home that evening, I got thinking, and my little business brain started ticking over. I realised that if I went out on my own to busk, I would be able to keep all of the money for myself. So, from then on, going out to sing became a regular weekend occurrence. True, earning some pocket money was a great motivator, but I also loved having the opportunity to perform. I found it a real challenge to see if I could manage to stop someone in their tracks and force them to listen to my voice; I found it a very satisfying experience to see the effect that I could have on them. There's a real sense of power from being able to do that with nothing except your voice.

As I write this now, I'm beginning to realise that I'm probably a bit of a show-off when it comes to singing. But you *have* to be to do my job. It would be very odd to be a full-time professional singer and to hate the idea of performing in front of a crowd. The more I busked, the more I discovered that I liked the attention that my singing brought me.

Soon, I decided to broaden my busking repertoire, by adding some tunes on my violin. I knew only a limited number of songs, so the instrumental pieces helped to pad out my set. I soon realised, though, that the crowds would disappear when I played the violin and reappear when I started to sing again. The violin swiftly became a former part of my act and I stuck to singing all the way through. There was nothing for it: I was simply going to have to learn some more songs.

I had already mastered the songs I had learned as part of the opera chorus. Now, I added a few Andrew Lloyd Webber numbers as well, including the 'Pie Jesu' from his *Requiem*. Since then, I've sung that song so many times in so many different places around the world that I'm giving it a rest from my repertoire at the moment. For me, it will always be one of the songs I associate with my period of starting out on my career.

Conversely, I still enjoy performing 'Pokarekare Ana', which has become my signature song. It has taken me all across the world and I've performed it for so many different people. It's a song that has stuck by me throughout and it's always a crowd pleaser. I regard it as being my trusty old faithful.

When I started busking regularly, it was not really something that kids did in New Zealand. It was more for hippies doing their juggling and circus acts, or for music students in their twenties. The only youngsters out performing were the little violinists who had studied under the Suzuki method. There always seemed to be a lot of them, but there were no other kids out there singing regularly. Recently, I've noticed that there have been a far higher number of young buskers around the centre of Christchurch, so maybe it has become the 'in' thing to do over the past few years.

The area in which I used to busk was in Christchurch's tourist heartland and there must be many people who visited the city around the turn of the millennium who have videos of some of my earliest public performances sitting gathering dust on their shelves at home. I think it's probably best for all of us if these 'gems' remain as part of their private collections!

Street crowds can be tough to work because they are not paying upfront to see you. There's no expectation on their part that you will be good and, as they have made no direct financial investment in your act, they don't automatically have a connection with you. You do have to hook them in – and I found that a real challenge. Having said that, though, I do miss the challenge. These days, I do a concert and everyone is paying money to see me perform, so there's a very real pressure on me to ensure that I give a good show. Everyone has an expectation of what I'm going to perform, how I'm going to sound and what the show is going to be like. When you are busking and you sing a bum note, everyone is far more forgiving because you are giving them a free concert anyway.

I used to like to watch and interact with the audience and I would try to keep them listening for as long as I possibly could. If I could make someone who was out shopping stand in front of me and listen for half an hour, then that was a real achievement. Performing in front of crowds in the street is like taking part in a constantly changing popularity poll. If you do something that they don't like, they carry on with their lives and walk away. But, if they enjoy your act, then they hang around for more. At a paying concert, you don't get that sort of feedback. Nor would you sensibly want to provoke it, either!

Over time, I earned enough money to buy myself a mini-amplifier and a microphone. It was a step up from how I started – just me and my unamplified *a cappella* voice, with a hat sitting on the ground in front of me to collect the money. I then started to bring along the family CD player to plug into my amplifier. Now, not only was I able to amplify my voice, but I could also sing along to a backing track, so my weekly outings on to the streets turned into quite a big production number. It allowed me to widen my repertoire still further. I did keep some *a cappella* songs in the mix, because they seemed to go down with the crowd, but singing with a backing track made my song choices far less limited than they had been previously.

Around this time, I also developed a novel sideline as a singing telegram. It all came about through a family friend, Gavin Becker, who went by the professional name of Sunshine the Clown. We met him because Isaac had become fascinated with his balloon-making skills at the local mall. One of his business interests was running a singing-telegram service and, when he heard me sing, he invited me to work with him when the occasion demanded someone with a voice like mine. It was a bizarre experience for everyone involved. Gavin would turn up at some poor, unsuspecting victim's home dressed in a gorilla suit, with me standing next to him. The general idea was that he would scare them and I would sing to them. Often, I would sing personalised lyrics that Gavin had written to the tunes of well-known songs.

Not all of our singing telegrams were quite like this, though: some of them could be quite touching. On one occasion, Gavin sent me to see one of his best friends, who was celebrating her birthday. I presented her with a huge bunch of her favourite flowers and then sang 'Somewhere Over the Rainbow'. She was blown away by his thoughtfulness and became very emotional, bursting into tears.

Although the busking was taking up a lot of my spare time at weekends, it didn't stop me from broadening my horizons into the world of musical theatre. The first hurdle was always getting through the audition process. The whole family would keep an eye out for the audition notices in the local newspaper. After applying, I would usually find myself being called in as part of a group of ten or twelve youngsters and we would each have a go at some of the singing for the specific role.

My first straight acting role came in *The Darling Buds of May*. It was not something I would usually have considered, because there were no singing roles, but I was good friends with our neighbours, Emma Ritchie, who is a couple of years older than me, and her sister, Nicola, who is a year younger than me. I knew Nicola particularly well because we often shared the same roles. In professional productions, child actors tend to work for only half the productions, and so Nicola and I were often picked for the same role in alternate performances. We shared the role of Marta in *The Sound of Music* and also of Tiny Tim in *A Christmas Carol*. The two girls were both also in Canterbury Opera Youth. Nicola and I look so similar that on one occasion her grandmother mistakenly thought a photograph of me in the local paper in full costume was actually her granddaughter.

The auditions took place one evening after Canterbury Opera Youth and, as the Ritchies often gave me a lift home, I had to wait around for them. I was already there so there was no point in just being a bystander and I decided to give it a go. Without really meaning to, I got the part.

As Sophie and Isaac became older, we quite often found all three of us in the same productions. When we were in *Rush*, a gold-mining-themed musical, our parents' stamina was tested to the limit. Sophie and I were in one cast, but Isaac was put in the alternate cast. This meant that Mum and Dad had to spend every night of the run ferrying us to and from the theatre without a single day's break.

I loved being in the musicals because not only did I get the chance to sing but there was also an opportunity to act and dance. It's easy to forget, but it gave us a tremendous social life outside school as well. During rehearsals, I would always take along a pack of cards in my bag and would sit playing Fish or Uno with my friends at the back of the hall when we were not needed on stage. We tended to bump into the same people at each new production, so, instead of spending the evenings and weekends hanging out at friends' houses, I would meet my friends at rehearsals and during performances.

There was a great attraction in having that easy way of socialising. I had decided not to audition for a part in *The King and I* so that I could concentrate on my schoolwork. Then, I went along to one of the auditions and saw so many of my friends whom I had met in other musicals that I instantly changed my mind and went for a part.

I loved getting dressed up before each performance and, when the curtain went up, I felt a huge adrenalin rush; it's a mixture of apprehension, nerves and excitement. Every time you perform on a live stage, you are laying yourself open to things going wrong – that is the scary bit. But, when things go right and you leave the audience happy, or you even move them to their feet, then that is one of the most fantastic feelings in the world.

There was a spell when, much to my consternation, I seemed to be offered only boys' roles. I never imagined that I would get a male role in a run of *The Nutcracker* by the Royal New Zealand Ballet. After all, this surely would be an opportunity for me to wear a beautiful sparkly pink dress and dance around the stage looking every inch the ballet queen. The problem was that there were scores of girls and very few boys auditioning for the child roles and ultimately the five girl parts and the five boy parts were shared out among ten girls. You've guessed it already: I was chosen as one of the five who had to wear a horrible itchy wig and a suit. All we could do was look on enviously at the other five girls, who wore shiny dresses completely covered in jewels. We were all very jealous. To add insult to injury, when I was not dressed up as a boy, I had to play the part of a rat. This was not the result I had imagined when I went along to the audition.

I had only recently played Tiny Tim in *A Christmas Carol*, where I spent the whole time dressed in a boy's suit and leaning on a crutch. It happened again with a performance of *Snow White and the Seven Dwarfs*. Don't ask me why – and please excuse the pun – but the only reason I was even considered for a role was because they were one dwarf short.

It was a production by a professional Australian touring company and, for some reason that escapes me now, they were missing one of the little guys. The first I knew of it was when Mum arrived in school to explain the situation. My ballet teacher had some dancers performing in the show and suggested that Sophie and I alternate in the part of one of the dwarfs, as an emergency replacement.

The reason why Mum had to come to pick us up early from school was that the first performance was that very evening. I had the opportunity to join a rehearsal that afternoon, which Sophie watched. The following night, she had to go on stage without any rehearsal. It was all a bit of a blur for both of us, as you can imagine. Luckily, they gave us the role of Sleepy, so that we could fall fast asleep if we forgot our lines.

One of the first things that I noticed as I stood in line with my six new best friends was that I was by far the tallest of all of the dwarfs. The other six were very welcoming but very laid back about the whole thing. I, on the other hand, was very scared. I was always a skinny child, so, to make me look more like the other six, the costume people stuffed padding up the front of my shirt because I needed to develop a beer belly fast. It was certainly one of the more bizarre situations that I've found myself in.

There are a variety of talent agencies in Christchurch who are always looking for new people to put on their books. In 1996, when I was still only nine years old, I signed up to the

Spotlight Modelling Agency. I thought that the idea of having my photograph in a clothing catalogue was wildly exciting at the time and this was my goal.

Soon, I found myself starring in a commercial for the New World supermarket chain. Well, when I say 'starring', I might just be stretching the truth a little. My job was to splash around in a swimming pool with a boy of about my age. It had to look to the television viewers as if we were both having an amazing amount of fun in the summer sunshine. The trouble was that, to have a commercial ready for broadcast at the beginning of summer, you need to film it in the depths of winter. The pool was unheated and the water was absolutely freezing. The director kept encouraging us to look as if we were having the time of our lives, as we flailed about in the icy water, desperately hoping that he would get the shot he needed in as short a time as possible.

There were bright lights and reflectors all around the pool and on television it certainly looked as if we were enjoying ourselves in the summer sunshine, but the reality was very different. We stood huddled together wrapped in towels while the crew got everything together, before plunging into the water at the last possible moment and pretending to be happy. I could feel my body starting to go numb by the end. It taught me the lesson that not every job in show business is necessarily the right job for every individual. I've never been the strongest swimmer and, as I was being filmed, I kept on wondering how they were possibly going to make us look as if we were having fun. There must have been dozens of other kids who would have been better at the job than I was. Some of them may even have been used to swimming in cold water. I know that it makes me a bit of a wimp, but, in my defence, I was resolute enough to carry on with the job until the bitter end.

Working for New World has become a bit of a family tradition for the Westenras. Isaac was chosen to be 'the New

World Boy', which meant that he appeared in all of their advertising for a couple of years. He was everywhere you looked: in the corners of leaflets that fell out of the newspaper, on the covers of coupon books that were dropped into mailboxes and on posters all around the stores. Sophie never actually did any work for New World, but she too was successful in doing some modelling work and she also appeared in a television commercial, although it was nowhere near as chilly an experience as mine.

I very nearly won a role in an Australian film called *Amy*. Had I got the part, life might have turned out very differently for me. They had auditioned for the lead across Australia and New Zealand, as well as in England. I went along to the auditions in Christchurch, but they had also seen girls in Wellington and Auckland, so it was a tough competition. In the end, it came down to me, a girl from Sydney and a girl from Auckland, who were still in contention for the role. The producers took a long time to decide and I spent a whole summer waiting on tenterhooks. It was horrible to be left dangling. It was all the more frustrating because it was something that I really wanted to do: the lead role in a big film that involved a mixture of singing and acting – and that really appealed. I was still in my phase of wanting to be an actor, so, when they finally told me that I had not been given the part, I was really upset. When you're left waiting for so long, expectation builds and you start to imagine how the future might turn out in a particular way. Looking back on it now, though, I'm proud that everything didn't automatically go my way when I was younger. It's definitely good to make mistakes and have some knock-backs. I'm a firm believer that it's beneficial to be shaken up a bit because, if you have a really smooth ride all of the time, there's a danger that, when it really does matter, you might mess up.

I've always learned from the little mistakes I've made and setbacks I've faced along the way. For example, I was taught a valuable lesson when I was at the Talent Quest, where the music was so quiet that I couldn't hear it at the start of my song. Ever since, I've always insisted on a soundcheck first when I'm performing, just so that I can be sure of what's going on. I guess the whole journey taken by anyone who performs as a career is one big learning curve. Having knock-backs or being turned down for something you want is good for you. It builds your determination and it gives you an insight into how tough the real world can be.

My first experience of being on a television programme came on the very popular kids' show *What Now?* It was way before I had made my CDs and I just happened to be one of the kids sitting in the crowd. I was thrilled to be chosen to take part in one of the on-screen competitions. Using only my mouth, I had to grab as many apples out of a bowl of water as I possibly could within a time limit. I was up against a boy of around my age and, frankly, competitive Hayley kicked in. I was a girl on a mission. There was no way on earth that I was going to allow him to beat me. The highlight of the show for me was sitting in the gunge tank and being covered from head to toe in brightly coloured sticky liquid. Crazily enough, this was my prize for winning the silly apple competition. The show is still as popular now as it ever was and Sophie can often be seen working in the background on the show as a telephone operator, answering the phones.

My first big performance on television came a little later, as part of the McDonald's *Young Entertainers* contest. I had a secret yearning to be part of the Super Troupe – a group of kids who were on the show each week performing song-and-dance routines. In fact, it was more than a yearning. To be honest, I was desperate to be one of them, as would any kid be who loved to perform. As I sat at home watching, it always looked as if they were having so much fun. It was my ultimate ambition at the time: as a Super

Troupe member, I would be on television each week; I would perform songs to the nation each week; and I would get to dress up for the cameras each week. To my mind, it was the height of cool. But there was one big problem: I lived in Christchurch on the South Island and the show came from Auckland on the North Island. Unfortunately for me, most of the television companies and the biggest shows were based in the wrong part of New Zealand. It was simply too far for me to travel.

But there was a way that I could appear on the show. The Super Troupe might be on the show each week, but in reality, they were only the warm-up act to the main event: the televised talent competition. When the auditions for the show came to Christchurch, I leaped at the chance to give it a go. The first round of auditions was held in a village hall. It was not a particularly special venue and it didn't feel particularly 'showbiz', but there were a couple of cameras there filming everything we did.

I was chosen to move on to the heats. This was where things started to take a distinctly more glitzy turn. Mum was determined that I would look my best. Sophie and I were friends with two sisters from ballet, Emma and Lucy Carter, who were each the same age as we were. Mum became good friends with their mother, Martine, and it was to her that Mum turned for help in designing the dress for me to wear on my big television appearance.

As usual, Mum put a lot of effort into my costume. It was based on a light-blue ballet skirt with a handkerchief hemline. My top was covered in sequins. In the process of deciding on the final design, Mum had spent days bringing home different samples of cloth for me to look at. I was going to be on national television and it was a big deal. Thanks to Mum's hard work, I ended up with a fairy costume that was every little girl's dream. After the show was broadcast, one mother came up to me and said, 'My daughter loved watching you on TV. She kept on pointing at you and calling you a fairy.'

I felt like a princess in my sparkly costume and the final fitting helped add to the sense of anticipation ahead of the big performance, which was to take place at the Palms Shopping Centre. When I turned up at the mall, I was rushed away to have my hair done in ringlets by the hair and makeup people. I discovered for the first time what this process was like. Initially, the idea of having a professional make you look beautiful is exciting, but I found that for someone like me, who always wants to be in control, it can quickly turn into a bit of a nightmare. I've discovered since that this is particularly the case when I work with a hair or makeup artist for the first time. I'm never quite sure how it's going to end up. On this occasion, I was quite concerned about the amount of product they slapped into my hair. I realised that I was completely in their hands and, if it turned out in a way that I didn't like, then I was going to be able to do absolutely nothing about it.

While I waited to go on stage, everyone fussed around me. This was the first time I had been made to feel like a star. A lot of time and effort had been put into how I looked. I felt very special as I was escorted from the mall offices to the stage, which was surrounded by great big cameras. They even had one on a crane. I sang 'Walking in the Air' and I worked in a short ballet influenced dance. I was very proud that I had choreographed the entire thing all by myself. I was even more proud when my performance went down a storm, propelling me on to the semifinals.

As usual, my performance in the heats was a big Westenra family outing and quite a few friends came along too. I'm very lucky that Mum, Dad, Sophie and Isaac are so supportive of what I do. They come along to *everything*. As my brother and sister have become older and started performing themselves, the same rule holds true. When I go back home, I'm always there with Mum and Dad, cheering them on. We are a close bunch and the thought of the family splitting up for big events such as Christmas would be crazy. I automatically go home for the holidays even now.

My performance was well received by the judges, one of whom was our local wizard, a Merlin-type figure, who regularly performed in the square by Christchurch Cathedral. He has become very well known over the years, and, even now, tourists who have been to Christchurch still ask me, 'Is the wizard still in the square?'

I must have cast something of a spell on him, because he gave me a really high score, saying that my performance reminded him of 'fairies and elves'. It propelled me through to the next round and I felt as if I was now well and truly on a big show-business adventure.

One of the people who saw the broadcast of the heat was Alan Traill, who was to become an enormous influence on my career. He is a very successful Christchurch businessman, who owns the franchises for around half a dozen McDonald's restaurants in the city. He invited the whole Westenra family out to dinner at one of his restaurants because there were only a few people from Christchurch who had made it into the main part of the competition.

From the start, Alan and his wife Nettie were as supportive as it was possible to be. We arrived at the restaurant to find a big yellow balloon with the words 'Good Luck Hayley' on it. Alan is a very well-spoken man and thoughtful in the truest sense of the word, in that he's careful and measured in everything he says. I was very touched when he turned to me at the end of the meal and said, 'Even if you get no further than this, you should be so proud of coming this far.'

After having known me for a couple of years, Alan gave me a VIP card, which was a big hit with my friends.

'Not many people have this card,' he said as he handed it over.

The card read, 'This card entitles Hayley Westenra and a friend to a free meal of their choice at McDonald's.'

From then on, if we were hanging out in the mall, one of my friends would say to me, 'Hey, Hayley, let's grab something to eat at the food court. And what about that card you have?' We would then share out the food between us.

There were not very many of these cards in existence. The only other ones I knew about were given by Alan to the players for the Crusaders, the Canterbury rugby team. On one occasion, I went into a McDonald's restaurant that it turned out that Alan didn't own and tried to use the card. Everyone behind the counter looked a little confused, but they still handed over the free meals, even though they had a suspicious look in their eyes. Only afterwards did I discover that it was not one of Alan's restaurants and this was the reason for the blank faces. Still, I managed to score myself a couple of free meals in the process!

For the semifinals in Taupo, I sang Andrew Lloyd Webber's 'Wishing You Were Somewhere Here Again'. Unfortunately for me, things did not go quite so smoothly as my performance in the heats. As I was singing, I lost control of my voice and ended up with a frog in my throat on one of my first notes. As far as I was concerned, I had completely messed up. After I had finished, I stood back-stage shaking from the experience. It seemed to me at the time to be the most horrific thing that had ever happened to me in my whole life. I was still young and, as I waited to hear the views of the judges, the mistake was gradually amplified out of all proportion in my mind. It was such a big deal for me: I was in the semifinals; it was on national television; I had embarrassed myself; the judges would never know just how well I could sing. I was convinced that one of the other two acts I was up against – a dancer and a flautist – would go through.

The host, Jason Gunn, walked up to me. I had met him a couple of times before at local events. He was very encouraging and tried to comfort me by saying, 'The judges know your potential and what you're capable of.'

I didn't share his optimism. But somehow – and to this day I'll never know quite how – I made it through to the final. When my name was read out, I was completely taken aback. I felt quite undeserving of it all because, as far as I was concerned, I had stuffed up my performance. But the judges must have backed me because they had heard me in rehearsals earlier in the day. They saw past the frog in my throat and put me through.

When the day of the finals arrived, I discovered that I was the only solo act. There were a couple of family-based dance troupes, four singing brothers and me. There were no problems this time and my performance went well, but, then, so did everyone else's. It was a hard job for the judges to compare singers with dancers and groups with a solo act. They gave me a huge amount of positive feedback after I had performed my piece, 'The Mists of Islay'. Ultimately, I came in at fourth position out of the four acts, but I was overjoyed to have made it to the final. My only disappointment came because I had hoped to give something back to my family. The first two prizes were family holidays and it would have been great to have taken everyone away on a luxury trip because they were there with me on the whole journey, helping to support me along the way. It would have been really cool to have been able to say, 'Hey, guys! I won you a family holiday!'

In the end, I won a mountain bike and a helmet, which was not quite the same thing.

CHAPTER 5
GETTING SERIOUS

My career as a recording artist began thanks to a guy from Rotorua, who had heard me singing on the McDonald's *Young Entertainers* show. After each TV performance he used to send me a postcard congratulating me on my success at getting through to the next stage. After the final, he sent me one last card and at the end wrote, 'I would love to have a recording of the three songs that you performed on the programme. Is this possible? I'm more than happy to send a blank tape to you and to pay for any incurred costs.'

At home, we didn't have any recording devices, but the suggestion set me thinking that it would be quite a cool idea to make a recording. The seed was planted. I was due to go to a studio shortly afterwards to make a short recording for a millennium concert that was coming up.

'You should ask the engineer whether he's got any free time for recording – and what the deal is,' said Mum, as I left home to go to the studio.

So I did.

'Well, I haven't got any work on over the holidays, so that could be quite a good time to do it,' came the unexpectedly positive reply. It would cost us NZ$80 per hour to hire the studio and the engineer (which is quite a bit cheaper than it costs me these days with Decca, I can tell you!).

Eighty dollars an hour was a lot of money for us, but I paid for the recording out of the money that I had saved from busking. I've always been a saver rather than a spender and would always squirrel away any birthday or Christmas money in my piggy bank, rather than splurge it on some new toy. To this day, I love nothing better than discovering a good bargain, especially when it comes to clothes and disposable things. I'm very conscious of the value of money. I do occasionally have a moment when I splurge these days, but I usually feel guilty about it afterwards. Any high-priced items tend to be work-related. Recently, I spent an awful lot of money on an amazing dress to wear on stage, but I was able to justify the expenditure to myself because I owe it to the people who have paid a lot of money to come to my concerts to appear in a nice gown.

But, aside from things that are work-related, I never think, Oh, I've *got* to have that! I'm not a big jewellery girl and I'm quite happy with bargain trinkets from accessory shops. The only things where I don't tend to look at the price are related to staying healthy. I'm happy to spend the extra for fresh organic food and I see health supplements as an investment rather than a luxury. I did pay for a course of acupuncture recently, which was not cheap, but I felt that it was worth it if it was going to help me to stay healthy. I certainly don't feel that spending money on manicures or pedicures is justified. I've had a couple in the past and, each time, I've walked out of the salon questioning why I had just spent £30 for a lady to smile at me sweetly and buff my nails – something that I could have done perfectly well myself.

So, although the studio costs seemed expensive, I didn't regard making a CD as an unnecessary luxury. It seemed like a sensible thing for me to be spending my money on at the time. As it turned out, it was probably the best investment that I'll ever make in my life.

I had kept the backing music for the songs that I had performed on the programme. The tracks had been especially created for the show and, because of that, each song was just a two-minute burst, all chopped down for television timing.

A time was booked in the studio with the very helpful recording engineer, Rob Mayes. I had intended to record only the three songs from the television show plus a couple more for which I had found some backing music. Rob was very encouraging and suggested that I record a few more tracks so that I would be able to leave with a complete album.

The challenge was to find suitable backing music to enable me to take up his suggestion. It was a mission! I spent hours going through my karaoke CDs finding songs. Some of the tracks for which I did find music didn't really seem suitable for me to sing, so the quest would go on. Basically, I was deciding the contents of this first album on the availability of backing music, rather than because I felt passionate about a particular song. We were thrilled to discover some downloadable midi files on the Internet, but would then have to reject them because they had a tacky drum beat or terrible keyboard playing. It became hugely frustrating, but it did make for an album with enormous variety in the end.

I was especially pleased to discover a version of the Bee Gees' 'How Deep is Your Love?' that I could use. I listened to it over and over again and worked hard to build up the harmonies. When it came to recording, I sang all of the different versions, and Rob then multitracked these and mixed them together, so at one stage there were three of me singing simultaneous harmonies. It was very exciting and high-tech, compared with what I had been used to. I felt very grown up, like a real recording star.

When the recording session was over, we designed a cover that included a photograph of me taken by Mum and my name, 'Hayley Dee Westenra'. I've no idea why we included my middle name. It's the only time it has ever appeared on the front of one of my albums and I can assure you that it will never appear again. It was very homemade-looking, but we were all very proud of it.

The demand for a recording of me singing from passers-by on the streets when I was out busking was getting louder. One lady came up to me at the end of a song and asked, 'Have you done a recording of your voice?'

'Actually, I have – just recently,' I replied. I wanted to continue with my singing and so directed her over to Mum, hoping that she would explain. I didn't realise that she had a copy in her bag, but apparently the lady begged Mum to allow her to buy the copy from her. Mum was reluctant to sell one to a stranger because she had so few copies in the first place. We had made only enough to give to close family and friends.

One of the people we did have a copy for was Alan Traill, who had continued to be very supportive of me ever since the McDonald's *Young Entertainers* contest. While we were at his house, we mentioned in passing that we were looking to get a large number of copies produced professionally, but that it was probably going to cost too much.

Later that evening, he came around to our house and knocked on the door. After we had welcomed him inside he astounded us with what he had to say next.

'Look, I've been thinking about this. You really should get this album produced professionally. I really want you to get it done. Here's the money. If you pay me back, great. But, if you can't, then no worries.'

He then presented me with a NZ$5,000 cheque. Despite our protestations that he was being too generous, he made it clear that it was a loan that we could pay back. I was completely blown away by his generosity. So were Mum and Dad. Once we had accepted his offer, we had no excuses not to go ahead with making an album. I was taken aback by Alan's belief in my ability. He was the first person outside my family to believe in me so much that they were actually prepared to invest their own money in me. Without a doubt, his decision left an imprint on me, giving me a little bit more confidence in myself.

As soon as the decision had been made, we plunged into album-making mode. Mum did most of the negotiations – and you have to remember that my family were not steeped in the traditions and practices of the music business. Everything we did and everything we discovered was absolutely brand new to us. Mum found out how the whole process of manufacturing a significant number of CDs works. She learned how we would need to pay for a glass master to be created, from which all of the copies would be made. She was told that, if you are going to the expense of making a glass master to run off five hundred copies, you might as well manufacture a thousand copies because the increase in cost at that stage is going to be relatively small. So, we decided to produce a thousand CDs, which is quite a lot to sell in anyone's book, but we were determined to find a way of shifting them and recouping the money.

One of the earliest decisions was that we would change the album's name. So, much to my relief, out went 'Hayley Dee Westenra' and in came 'Hayley Westenra – *Walking in the Air*'.

As well as manufacturing the CD, we needed to come up with a more professional-looking photograph for the cover, rather than one that had been borrowed from the family album. Mum's first idea was for us to go out to the beach and take a photograph of me among the tussocks in the mist. Early one morning, she set off for a recce and discovered the perfect spot with the requisite amount of mist. She started speaking to a woman walking her dog nearby and asked her if the weather that morning was typical.

'I've been living here for the last ten years and it's only the third time that I've seen mist' came the disheartening reply.

The following morning the whole family packed up the car and headed out to the beach in search of mist. We set off very early to try to catch that moment when the sun was bright, but not quite hot enough to burn off the mist. It was not to be, though, and, when we arrived, there was no mist to be seen anywhere, despite our best efforts to find some. In the end, we gave up on the idea altogether and took no photos at all. Instead, we sat having a picnic on the beach, eating the vegemite-and-cheese rolls that Mum had packed for our breakfast.

Ever resourceful, we took the opportunity to drive around Christchurch looking for places to take photos. Eventually, I found myself standing in my Great-Aunt Jo's donkey enclosure on her farmyard. Mum has a very strong photographic eye and is always on the lookout for interesting locations to frame pictures. She had discovered a moss-covered shed on the farm, which she thought would make a perfect setting. I gingerly tiptoed across the field to the shed, studiously trying to avoid sinking into the mud. Mum, on the other hand, couldn't have cared less whether her shoes became caked in mud. She was in creative mode, climbing everywhere in an attempt to get the angle and the light right for the big shot.

She took some great photos, one of which we used on the homemade poster that we produced to try to promote the album. Once the album was finished, we realised that it would take too long to make the money back if we relied only on the copies that we could sell while I was busking, so we journeyed around all of the Christchurch CD stores, befriending the managers and persuading them to order a few of the CDs each.

It was still a very small enterprise, but a track from the record was played on the local radio station Plains FM. It was the first time that I had received any radio airplay for a song that I had sung. I was also featured on CTV, the local television station, which broadcasts across Christchurch.

Interest was growing and so we speculatively sent a copy of the CD to each of the big record companies in Auckland. Enough people seemed to be keen on the album and we began to wonder if it might have a life beyond the CD players of Christchurch.

Gray Bartlett has had a very successful career in New Zealand as an agent and as a musician, and my appearance on CTV caught the attention of one of his colleagues. She phoned us up and suggested we send him a copy of the album. Gray then mentioned me to George Ash, who was the man in charge of Universal Music New Zealand, one of the country's music industry big hitters.

'Yes, we've been sent her album, we've been thinking about bringing her to Auckland,' George said.

And then, before I really had any time to appreciate what was actually going on, I was being flown up to Auckland to record my first album. 'But they haven't even met me,' I said to Mum on the plane. All they had was a homemade demo CD and a handful of photographs taken by Mum. I still wonder whether they were in fact simply bringing me to Auckland to make a better-quality demo and whether I would have found myself on the next plane back to Christchurch, had it not turned out well.

It was all so sudden. Out of nowhere, I was being told, 'Yep, this is it. You're going to record your first album. Now, off you go to the studio.' It was exciting, surprising and completely overwhelming, although I always tried not to let it show on the outside. I found it quite an unnerving experience. Inside, I was thinking, Oh, but what if I'm not what they expect? What if they think I'm prettier than I am in reality? They had never even met me and I couldn't believe that they could possibly be flying me up there to give me a record contract and to make a proper, professional album.

Back then, I was not quite as aware as I am now of the need for an artist to have an image – to look and dress a certain way. I thought my voice would carry me. I was aware that image came into it and was a part of the package, but I was more concerned that they were expecting me to be something or someone I was not, because they had never met me before. I realised that Auckland was a much bigger city than Christchurch and I think that in my head I had a picture of the sort of artist that big record companies would be looking for and I knew that I simply was not the sort of glitzy girl that they wanted. I suppose that I lacked confidence in everything except my singing ability.

The new CD was based on my family-produced *Walking in the Air* album, but I was very proud that new arrangements of songs were written especially for me. And I no longer had to use versions of the backing tracks that were just two minutes long. I didn't realise it at the time, but the process of making the CD was incredibly fast, barely lasting a couple of weeks. On some days, I was recording four songs from start to finish, but I knew no different, so I didn't question it or complain. I was just grateful to be there. I didn't know that the normal process of making an album can take weeks or even months and that this was an extraordinarily fast-turnaround album. I just assumed that the process of recording always happened like that.

I was so in awe of the whole situation. Not only did I record in a bigger and better recording studio, but I felt very glamorous trying on the different outfits that had been bought especially for me for my photo shoot. It was every girl's dream.

My lack of confidence also extended to speaking out creatively about the album. I was not convinced that anyone would listen to me if I told them that I thought that the 'Pie Jesu' needed to be slower, or if I felt that another track had been put into the wrong key. A keyboard track had already been recorded for all the songs as a guide and it didn't occur to me that, as the artist, I could put my foot down and get them to rerecord the keyboard part to follow me instead of me following the keyboard part. It was a very beneficial learning curve for me and, from that moment on, I vowed to become far more involved in the process on any subsequent albums that I made.

As a bonus track, Universal got hold of a recording of 'Amazing Grace' which I had performed with the Royal Scots Dragoon Guards when I was fourteen. They were in New Zealand on tour and I had joined them on stage in Hamilton. It was this recording that was used. One of the particular challenges I discovered was that bagpipes can play in only one key, which was, in truth, way too low for my voice. It was still an exciting performance and I think this comes across on the recording.

The album was very simply called *Hayley Westenra*. Once again, I had no high expectations of how many copies it might sell. For me, it seemed a great achievement for a teenage girl from Christchurch to have made an album like this, thanks, in the main, to the tenacity and support of her parents. I didn't know how many albums I would have to sell to make it a successful record or the number of sales that would render it a flop. I don't think the record company had enormously high expectations for it because they had never really had an artist like me before, so they didn't have any historical precedents to judge it by.

I was on the television programme *Sixty Minutes* on the Sunday night before the album was released. It's a big documentary-style programme, which covers three topics, spending around twenty minutes on each one. I was interviewed for the show and I can still remember the horror I felt when the producers told me that they wanted to have a shot of me at my piano in my bedroom. The whole camera crew squashed themselves into my little room. As I waited for them to set up the lights, I looked around the green wallpaper on the walls, covered with random pieces of artwork that I had painted myself. Jars filled with coloured stones, my collection of shells and various hand-painted pottery creations jostled for space on the shelves. It was just like any other teenage girl's bedroom, except that today, plonked right in the middle of it, were a camera crew with their bright lights and big sound boom.

I had not realised just how influential a programme *Sixty Minutes* is in New Zealand. They have continued to be incredibly supportive of me ever since. The morning after that first interview aired, there were apparently people queuing up outside the record shops in Christchurch, waiting to buy my CD. It was truly amazing. Suddenly, my album was selling faster than even my most optimistic supporter would have predicted. They were flying off the shelves and, in no time at all, the album had gone triple platinum in New Zealand.

A lot of the people who bought that first record were mothers and grandmothers, but these days I'm connecting with more people my own age as well. My albums always sell particularly strongly in the week before Mother's Day. As well as the older fans, I also seem to appeal to young girls who are themselves aspiring to be singers. These days, when I'm performing in New Zealand, I often look out into the audience and see three generations of families coming along to my concerts, which gives me a real buzz. To be honest, I don't mind at all who buys my records. I simply want to make music that connects with real people, no matter who they are or where they come from.

When people say to me that I'm the biggest name in New Zealand's recording history, I find it quite an incredible concept, in the truest sense of the word. I'm still very much focused on the simple things in life and in getting the basics of what I do absolutely right. Despite the fact that I now perform in front of thousands of people, I still want to give a performance that is just as authentic as those that I used to give in front of far smaller crowds. I still enjoy the same things and have the same group of friends I had before I had a number-one record. I love going to the movies and chatting to my family on the phone. I don't feel that I've changed that much. I'm still working on bettering my voice, finding great songs, and even writing songs for myself. These are the same things I've always spent my time doing. It's not as if my life had been tipped upside down. I feel as if I'm very much on the same path – just a bit further along it.

When *Hayley Westenra* went to number one, I took it completely in my stride. It didn't mean as much to me as it probably should have done. I guess the biggest change was at school, where other kids would notice me, saying, 'Hey! It's that singer. Oi, sing us a song!' Or they'd just whisper, 'Look, it's Hayley Westenra' as I went from one class to the next. I was very fortunate in that there was certainly no bullying at school, just joking around. In fact, the only time when I was bullied was far, far earlier, when I was around eight years old and I was hassled by a group of girls after I sang the Denice Williams song 'Let's Hear It for the Boy'. These girls used to tease me by saying, 'Who's your boy, then, Hayley?' I was only eight years old and unfortunately I didn't have any clever quips to fire back at them, so took the teasing to heart. It didn't last for long, though, and it would have better enabled me to handle any bullying as a teenager but thankfully none of any substance came my way.

Occasionally, the kids at school who didn't know me that well would try to wind me up, but it never bothered me in the slightest. My friends and I actually found it quite amusing and, in truth, I probably enjoyed the attention. When you've been on television, people start to notice you and it felt like a measurement of success. It seemed as though I was obviously getting somewhere because people were engaging with me. That said, I did realise that it was possible to be famous and not successful and understood the importance of having a record that was high in the charts.

I carried on with my classes, but, increasingly, I found myself spending more and more time promoting the album. I performed in a national tour across New Zealand, taking in places such as Wellington, Hamilton, Christchurch and even Timaru. It was very special to go back there for the first time as a professional singer. It was my grandparents' home town and never mind the fact that I might have sold more tickets in a bigger city. I just wanted to perform in Timaru because Nanna and Grandad were there.

One of the things that I've learned about the record industry is that, when things are going well, record companies always want more – and quickly. So I was asked to make a Christmas album, *My Gift to You*, a title that I have to confess I've always thought of as being rather cheesy.

Above: The littlest star: my performing debut, aged six
Below: Captivating the audience with my new microphone

Above: I loved my tutu, but ballet soon took second place to the singing
Below: Caroline Bay Carnival, January 1999

above: I have inherited my musicality from both my Nanna and Grandad
below: Busking for our lunch: Sophie, Isaac and me in the Arts Centre area of Christchurch

Above: The Pure tour, with Isaac, Sophie, Brandon Poe and Hinewehi Mohi

Left: Cadogan Hall

Above: Holding the American Society of Young Musicians Young Performer of the Year trophy
Below: Collecting another award at the New Zealand Music Awards

Above: Recording at Air Studios with Sir George Martin
Below: The photo that my mum took for the cover of my very first album

Above: Kathryn and me having a delirious moment due to serious jet lag in Japan!
Below: Filming a PBS special for American television with my sister Sophie

Left: At the Classical Brit Awards, 2006

Below: The Westenra family together for the launch of my album Odyssey

When you are a teenager, you are so conscious of not being 'cheesy', but, as I couldn't come up with anything better (bearing in mind the school year was coming to an end and my head was also trying to deal with maths sums and science equations), I let the title be. *My Gift to You* it was.

I recorded the album in less than a week. For the first time, I was allowed to have some say in the tracks that I recorded and I said no to 'Once in Royal David's City' and no to 'Away in a Manger'. What a thrill! The tracks were being decided upon while we were on the tour. One of the musicians supporting me, a violinist called Ben Morrison, was a friend from my class at school. When we were in Auckland, we had half an hour to spare after we had checked out of the hotel and were waiting for our ride, so Ben and I raced down to a local music store and flicked through the CDs there. Looking for inspiration on tracks that I could record for the Christmas album, I came across a Kathleen Battle CD of spirituals and, recognising the name, wondered if there would be something interesting on it. I asked the shopkeeper if I could have a listen to the disc. I skimmed through the tracks, stopping at one that grabbed me from the first few notes. It was called 'Mary Did You Know?' I loved the song the instant I heard it and I knew that I just had to sing it. I had never really felt that way about a song before. Previously, it had been a more matter-of-fact process, where I would agree that a song suited my voice and then we would record it.

For the first time, I had formed a real connection with a song and I was very excited about my discovery. I ran down Queen Street back to the hotel, album in hand, very eager to share my news. When the time came to make the final decisions about the Christmas CD, I knew that I wanted to include it more than any other track. It was my first editorial decision and it gave me a big boost in confidence when it became one of the big songs from the album.

Gaining confidence when you are working with recording-industry professionals is a very gradual process. With every album, I'm getting a little bit more confident. Other tracks on that album included 'You'll Never Walk Alone', which became one of my big live concert tracks, and 'Chestnuts Roasting on an Open Fire', which I enjoyed because it was slightly more like a pop song in its style – laid back, while retaining its original warmth and cosiness.

My Gift to You was the first album on which I sang new material that had been written especially for me, and that made me extremely proud of the opening track, 'All I Have to Give'. There were some old favourites, too: 'Somewhere Over the Rainbow', which I perfected as a singing telegram, and what has ended up becoming my signature song, 'Pokarekare Ana'. I was also really excited that the big bosses had let my sister Sophie, who was eleven at the time, sing backing vocals on two of the tracks, 'Do You Hear What I Hear?' and 'Through These Eyes'. We are so close that it was nice to be able to have her on the album. However, I was also quite nervous for her as well. During the recording, I enjoyed taking on the role of overprotective big sister, giving her encouragement and what little advice I had.

The process of making the album was slightly unusual. We were so tight for time that two producers were employed: David Selfe, who had made my first Universal album, and Jim Hall. Each was given half of the album to work on. Once I had finished working on all the tracks that Jim had pre-prepared, we still had one song to find. He picked up some songbooks in the studio and started to flick through them trying to find some inspiration. I watched over his shoulder.

'Oh, I know that one – "Morning Has Broken",' I said, just as he was about to turn the page past it.

So he picked up his guitar and I sang along as he strummed the accompaniment. We went straight into the studio and recorded it moments later. It was as quick as that – on the spot. It meant that my second Universal Music album was complete.

I was starting to get the hang of working in recording studios. I've never been one of those artists who have superstitions or rituals around going into the studio, but I do like to have some healthy snack food to munch on between takes to keep my energy levels up. I always take a little container of chopped vegetables and fruit – strawberries, carrot sticks, celery sticks, that sort of thing. I never eat dairy-based foods before singing because – and here I must apologise for the graphic detail – dairy tends to make you overproduce phlegm, which clogs your throat. There's a risk of your singing with a frog in your throat, which wouldn't be pleasant for either the singer or those people listening to the album.

These are the sorts of tips that I learned from Dame Malvina Major, who is one of New Zealand's greatest operatic stars. She gave me some lessons and I trusted her opinions completely. Dame Malvina passed on a lot of advice to me in terms of singing technique, which has remained with me ever since. It was a real privilege to be able to spend time with her because, up until that point, I had had lessons with various teachers, but I had never really felt confident in my singing technique. I was very much relying on my natural voice. Even now, I still believe that I've a lot more work to do on my voice and I'm looking forward to a quiet period in my schedule, when I can focus on my singing technique.

I immediately respected Dame Malvina. I was also a little bit scared of her at first because I had this record contract and I was selling albums. I wrongly assumed that she would be thinking to herself, Who *is* this girl? She's out making records, when she hasn't even done her studying yet.

But I needn't have worried. She was encouraging and supportive in every possible way. She gave me one particularly important piece of advice: 'Stay true to yourself.' She never pushed me down the classical route into opera and, at the same time, she didn't look down her nose at my classical-crossover record contract, either.

At one point, a friend of hers heard me sing and said, 'Rip up your record contract! Go and do your study! You have potential to be a great opera singer, but you'll never make it if you stick with your record contract.' He certainly was not a very open-minded man. Much to my annoyance, he nearly made me cry, because, yes, I'm quite a sensitive soul! I felt better when Dame Malvina called us up later that evening and told me to ignore what he had said and to keep on going.

CHAPTER 6
ON RECORD

The success of my first Universal album had excited everyone at the record company in New Zealand. George Ash moved to Australia to run Universal Music there but he worked with his successor, Adam Holt, to interest the international side of Universal in working with me.

Record companies can be complicated places with lots of different labels and companies operating under one umbrella organisation. Sometimes they compete and sometimes they work together. Sometimes they appear to work together but turn out to have been competing all along. Although Universal Music New Zealand is a massive company on its own turf, it's relatively small when it comes to the rest of the world. To have taken an album by one of its artists and marketed it to all of the other Universal Music record companies in each of the territories around the world would have been too great a risk for Universal Music New Zealand to have taken.

The international dimension came along in the shape of Costa Pilavachi, who, at the time, was president of Decca Music Group. He was also part of the umbrella Universal Music company, and his role was to develop artists who would make records that would sell in different territories around the world. Decca is one of the best loved and most respected classical-music labels, and has been home to many of the genre's greatest stars, such as the conductor Sir Georg Solti, who enjoyed a lifetime contract with them.

A copy of my debut self-titled album found its way to the Decca Music Group's headquarters in London. I believe it's Jean-Hughes Allard, working in the A&R (Artists and Repertoire) division, that I have to thank sincerely for this next development in my career. I'm told he was playing my disc in his office rather loudly, and it caught the attention of Costa Pilavachi, who was working in his office just down the corridor. He liked what he heard and immediately got in touch with Universal Music New Zealand. Although George Ash and Adam Holt were absolutely behind the idea of my working with Decca to move on to the international stage, the people at Decca still had to be convinced that I was a good investment and, rather than send an underling all the way from their headquarters in London, Costa himself flew thousands of miles down to New Zealand.

I was performing in a concert in Wellington and it was arranged that Costa would watch me sing before coming to see us at home in Christchurch afterwards. I met him briefly at the hotel. He seemed a very charming and stylish man, the sort of person whose authority you instantly recognise. He was just that sort of guy and I was in awe of him because I knew that he was a big shot from the UK.

When he flew down to Christchurch, it was a huge deal in the Westenra household. Mum put Dad in charge of organising a restaurant where we could take him out to dinner. He booked a place on the Strip in Christchurch, an area filled with lots of cafés, bars and restaurant. When Costa was picked up at the airport, we noticed that he had taken one of Christchurch's posh cabs.

Suddenly, Mum started to panic that the restaurant that we had booked was not posh enough. So, at the last minute, we changed the booking to an Italian place called Palazzo, which is one of Christchurch's smartest eateries and is well known for its extensive wine list. It was a stroke of genius and we all got on exceptionally well there. It turned into a very successful evening, which was a real relief for all of us.

Costa is a very cultured man and he charmed the restaurant owner when he came over to chat. The waitresses were very knowledgeable about the food and wine and Costa, who appeared to be a man who liked the finer things in life, really appreciated this. Throughout the meal, Mum, Dad and I gave each other little glances of approval. We were very pleased with ourselves that we had chosen the right restaurant.

Costa was very jovial and showed a lot of interest in the whole family, and he went out of his way to include Sophie and Isaac in the conversation. I could sense that Mum and Dad were warming to him as well, because he was interested in what my brother and sister had to say, as opposed to directing all his attention on me. Mum was very proud when he commented on the fact that we all looked like healthy children. It was something that she reminded everyone of regularly for some time afterwards!

Costa also came to visit us at home and this was the cue for even more nervousness from the Westenras. I have to admit that I was really embarrassed about his coming to see our house because I assumed that he had been to the absolute top places around the world. Here was this international record-company big shot coming to little old Hayley's home, a regular house in Christchurch, with clutter all around the place – even though as many of the offending items as possible had been put away out of sight before his arrival.

Looking back on it, I realise I probably shouldn't have felt like that. I'm much more comfortable with who I am and where I've come from these days. And it didn't seem to make a difference to Costa what sort of house we lived in. He made everybody feel very much at home, which was odd because we actually were at home and he was the visitor.

Now that I've travelled around the world, I've seen the sorts of houses in which people live in other countries and I've come to realise how lucky we are in New Zealand. In fact, our home in Christchurch is in a beautiful location, with a large backyard in a grassy area surrounded by trees. It may not be a mansion in New Zealand terms, but it's huge compared with the space that most people have in a city such as London and it's absolutely massive compared with the space in which people live in somewhere far more densely populated, such as Hong Kong.

Now, I can understand that I should not have been embarrassed at all because there's nothing wrong with our house. But, at the time, I just assumed that Costa was going to be kind of disappointed in it.

Mum really picked up on Costa's view that I should not just be plucked out of my family unit and flown halfway around the world. Instead, he stressed how important it would be for the whole family to be involved. This reassured

Mum, since it had been something that had been gnawing away at her.

It was a pretty big thing for me to be working with Universal Music New Zealand, but then, suddenly, here was this global record company showing an interest. To be honest with you, in my naivety, I didn't realise its significance. I just assumed that the next step for everyone who had made an album was to move on to an international release. I was not aware that a local Universal Music company couldn't finance that and it was unlikely to happen without help from the international part of the company. I just assumed that the album would be handed over to other companies and somehow I would find myself on the other side of the world.

Costa flew home and he must have liked what he had seen, because, shortly afterwards, the deal was done between Decca Music Group and Universal New Zealand. I was lucky enough to become a Decca artist, which is an amazing privilege, because it's a record company that can really make things happen for an artist.

The deal was done in the background. I must admit that I was not really aware of all the negotiations that were happening between Universal Music in New Zealand and Decca. Before I knew it, I had a contract. We employed a music-industry lawyer, Campbell Smith, to go through the terms. When it came to actually signing the deal, I had to sit in the Universal Music offices with a massive document in front of me, every page of which had to be initialled. Campbell had been impressed by the fact that, at our previous meeting, I was asking questions about the contract as he went through it with me, but really I was not that interested at all. I was just being polite! I trusted my lawyer to look out for my best interests.

All I was excited about was making music and recording albums. I had been offered a five-album deal, which, although it sounds amazing, is actually fairly standard in the record industry. What tends to be missed out from the press releases that announce these deals is the absolute certainty that, if the first album doesn't sell enough copies, the other four will fail to materialise. I was not really worried about how much money I would earn from the contract, or for how long it was tying me to Decca. However, I did realise fairly quickly that it's the artist who tends to pay for everything. My parents have always been good at explaining things to me. They have never treated me like a child, so I've always been aware of how the financial side of things is structured.

Signing to Decca created one particularly big change for me. I would need to spend a lot of time away from home, both to make the album and then to promote it. There would be an awful lot of travel and so many different hotels in so many different cities, in every conceivable time zone, that I would lose count. It seemed like a fantastic adventure.

It would create a challenge for us as a family. Either Mum or Dad would need to travel with me as a chaperone, leaving the other parent to look after Sophie and Isaac, back at home. Mum travelled with me on our first trip to London. We would be away for a few months, so it was a real wrench leaving the other three behind. I chatted excitedly to the lady at the check-in desk, telling her where we were off to, and she wished me luck. Dad, Sophie and Isaac waved to us as we passed through the barriers into the departure lounge. Not long afterwards, we were sitting on an Air New Zealand plane as it taxied down the runway. I turned to Mum and said, 'Oh my gosh! This is it!'

It was my first big trip overseas. Previously, I had only ever been to Australia a couple of times for concerts and once to Hawaii as a three-year-old, when Dad had won a trip in a competition. Otherwise, the North Island was the extent of my travelling horizons. Usually, our holidays were local camping trips. Many families went to Australia for regular holidays but for us the money was spent on things such as music and ballet lessons.

I noticed that we had been put in business class on the plane, which made the whole flight even more exciting. I was not sad to be leaving – it was the beginning of a whole new adventure. I loved the service on the plane. It's something I still enjoy now. Although I'm usually a very careful eater, I said yes to everything that was offered to me: the nuts with the drinks, all of the meals, the dessert, the cheese and even the chocolate. I was relishing the whole experience.

I started to appreciate just how far away New Zealand was from the rest of the world. It was a long flight, which we broke up with an overnight stay in Los Angeles. While we were there, I became sick and ended up with a sore throat. I think that the initial excitement had evaporated slightly and I was starting to become nervous about what was to come. Because my throat was not feeling great, I became even more stressed. After all, I was about to meet the people from my record company for the first time and would need to perform for them. I also had only a hazy idea of what would be happening to me over the next few months and that added to the nerves.

We were in LA for the first time and I've taken a few years to warm to the city because of this initial experience. We were staying at an airport hotel, which was not great, and I was feeling sick. Mum and I decided to go for a walk to take in some fresh air. We have since learned that walking around this area of LA is simply not the done thing and we were a little confused as to why cars kept tooting at us.

We went back to the hotel and the restaurants were shut. We needed some food, but were reluctant to order room service because it looked so expensive. In the end, I ate a bowl of onion soup, which had way too much salt in it. It did nothing to alleviate my glumness. Only recently have I come to terms with the price of room service. I've now actually got over the fact that sometimes it's going to be expensive. At the end of the day, you've got to eat. I used to worry about it, but now I've become a little more relaxed about the whole thing.

When I stayed in foreign cities, I used to avoid eating out at restaurants as well because they were so expensive. Instead, I would go to the supermarket and make up my own meal from what I could find on the shelves there. It probably came to more than the price of a meal at the hotel in the first place.

The following morning, we boarded another plane for the final leg of the flight to London. I was feeling rather miserable because my throat was still playing up. I was increasingly stressed about what was to come. My mood didn't improve when we landed at a freezing cold Heathrow Airport and my mind drifted back to the lovely warm temperatures that we had left behind back home in Christ-church.

We were met at the airport and driven to a flat right opposite Decca's offices in west London. My mood lifted considerably. It was a beautiful place and JJ, a lovely man from Decca Music Group who had been put in charge of looking after us, had gone to a lot of trouble to make it seem welcoming for us, even putting a bag of chocolate Easter eggs in a bowl on the table and stocking the fridge with food for us. Although I had seen only very little of London, I was struck by how busy it seemed compared with home. The area around the flat struck me as being very cosmopolitan and exotic and my sense of adventure kicked back in. Things were looking up.

Mum and I had a great time in the flat. She would cook meals every evening, which we would eat in front of the television – we developed a real passion for British TV and we were already fans of *Coronation Street*, which runs back home. I became equally passionate about eating canned sticky-toffee pudding with milk poured over the top. British friends tell me this is a really weird thing to do and I should eat it with custard, but I enjoyed the contrast of the refreshing cold milk and the hot sticky-toffee pudding.

We loved spending my days off exploring the local shops. We had a habit of always converting the prices back to New Zealand dollars. Because the cost of living is far lower in Christchurch than it is in the centre of London, this meant that we would be able to justify buying only the very cheapest clothes, which didn't always look as great as they might have done. We loved visiting the charity shops. We call them 'op shops' back home – which is short for 'opportunity shops'. You might think that, with a new five-album international record deal, I would have spent my time buying up the latest fashions from *haute couture* boutiques, whereas, in reality, I spent hours searching out bargains, because everything seemed so expensive in London.

One of my early discoveries was the Tube. We don't have an underground system in Christchurch, so it was a real novelty. I was amazed by how easy it is to use and the fact that it will take you anywhere you want to go in London, once you have mastered the art of reading the map. It gave us the independence to go where we pleased around London, although we didn't have to use it twice a day, every day, in the rush hour. So I can appreciate that familiarity might breed contempt after a time.

I'm lucky enough to keep 'showbiz' hours, which tend to mean later starts and much later finishes than most workers, and, whenever I do have to join the commuters on their way to the office, I realise why so many people are not as enamoured with it as I had initially been.

Soon after I'd arrived in London, I was told about an important morning meeting. It was all very sudden and nobody had been talking about it. It just appeared out of the blue in my diary. For some reason, I didn't think that I needed to be there. Mum told me that I absolutely did have to attend. I rushed into the shower and was still getting dressed when one of the guys from the record company knocked on the door. I didn't quite understand why there was this sudden urgent need to get me to Decca's office, but all became clear when I walked through the door.

It was my birthday and everyone had gathered together in one room ready to surprise me with a party. I was so embarrassed because my hair was still wet and I was not looking in the least bit glamorous. It was very sweet of them, especially as I was so far away from home, although I've discovered since that, once you've been around for a while, record companies tend not to care quite so much about your birthday. When they are attempting to make a good impression at the beginning, they tend to try a bit harder.

The main reason for my having flown halfway around the world was, of course, for me to make my first album for Decca. Although London remained our base, the record company decided that I would make the album in Dublin with the producer Chris Neil and the Irish composer Ronan Hardiman. It was a wonderful creative process and I enjoyed working with both of them enormously. Working in the middle of the Irish countryside has its good and bad points. On the positive side, it's a beautiful country, with the friendliest people you could ever imagine. I also discovered the joys of Irish soda bread and, whenever I'm in Ireland now, I always have the most heavenly breakfast ever: Irish soda bread, a little butter and strawberry jam – it's the perfect way to start the day.

I also had my first experience of Guinness after both Chris and Ronan managed to persuade Mum and me how good it was for us. He told us that it used to be prescribed to pregnant women because it was high in iron. Anyway, we were easily convinced, so, at the end of each day's recording, I would drink half a pint of Guinness – purely for medicinal reasons, you understand. I still have the occasional half now, but I drink it with blackcurrant these days.

Working on the album was a real family effort and it was a lovely relaxed atmosphere. Ronan had two young children, Ellie and Sam, who were great to have around.

The downside was more due to location than anything else. We were stuck in a hotel in the middle of nowhere and the room service was very expensive. There was no super-market, so we were totally reliant on the hotel kitchens. The menus didn't change that much and living there for two months meant that things became a little monotonous on the culinary front – especially since both Mum and I are not big meat eaters. We would have much preferred to have been put in a little flat where we could have cooked meals for ourselves. It would have been much more our style. It really was not ideal and we felt completely cut off, with a long walk before the nearest stop for a bus to take us into town.

One of Chris Neil's greatest strengths was in picking songs. He found some really wonderful tracks such as 'River of Dreams' and 'Dark Waltz'. Over those two months in Ireland, we made an album, which I loved at the time. I was so excited about the whole concept of having my own new songs to work with. Another one of my favourites was 'Who Painted the Moon Black?', which was written by Sonia Aletta Nel, who comes from Namibia. I was really pleased with the album that we handed over to the record company. I had played some of the tracks to my friends back in New Zealand and they had thought that the album had a very cool, New Age vibe to it.

But the bosses didn't like it. It was a little bit too synthesised for the record company's tastes and it was not the classical-crossover album that they had imagined. There were a few more beats on the record than they might have expected and it was quite electronic-sounding in places. Now, with the benefit of hindsight, I understand completely why they made that decision and I agree totally with what they were saying. But, at the time, I was really disappointed because I had been psyching myself up for the album release. I had poured my heart and soul into everything that we had recorded and it was very hard to find that they had pulled the plug on it. It had been a real team effort for Chris, Ronan and me – so that made the whole thing that much more difficult to bear. They were perfect gentlemen throughout and there was no great falling out, but people who run record companies are paid to make tough decisions and the Decca bosses decided that I would completely remake the album with a new producer.

When I heard the news, I never reached the stage in my mind where I thought that it had all been in vain and that nothing would ever be released. However, I was impatient for people to hear what we had done. In reality, things moved on quite quickly, especially compared with how long some artists have to wait to have their albums released. But, at the time, I was so disappointed. There were no tears – just an immense feeling of frustration.

I did have faith that we would get there in the end.

CHAPTER 7
PURE

After a lot of thought, Decca decided that Giles Martin should be the producer of my first album for them. Mum and I met him for the first time in a café in the very trendy Notting Hill area of London. He was much younger, better-looking and more stylish than I had expected and I didn't quite know what to make of him at first. I gave him a Maori bone carving, designed to be worn around the neck as a pendant, which probably resulted in his not quite knowing what to make of me either. I explained to him what it was, but he seemed slightly bemused by it.

We stayed in London working for quite a few more months on *Pure* – this was the version of the album that would finally be released. Mum and Dad took it in turns to fly over to spend time looking after me. The album was recorded in two different London locations: Eastcote Studios in Ladbroke Grove and Air Studios in Hampstead. When I was going to Ladbroke Grove, I used to catch a No. 52 bus each morning. So, if you are reading this and you think that recording albums is all about glitzy locations, spacious limousines and flunkies to fulfil your every need, then you should think again. That scenario couldn't be further from the truth. I used to wear clothes designed for comfort rather than style: khaki army pants, white sneakers, a cap – all bought at a bargain price at a Kensington charity shop.

I liked those journeys to and from the studio on the bus because it meant that I could look at myself in the mirror each morning and honestly say that I was keeping it real. I was very conscious of not becoming too starry before I had actually done anything. Even though I was very young, I realised that there was a lot of hype around the music business and I promised myself that I would do everything I could not to become caught up in it. I was more than happy to walk to the bus stop and catch the bus to the studios with my little packed lunch under my arm each day. On the first day, my food included a hard-boiled egg, which stank out the studio. Giles told me how much he hated them. But he was a great joker and so I brought in a hard-boiled egg every single day, just to wind him up. Luckily, he saw the funny side!

On our days off, Mum and I would wander around Covent Garden market and discover London. But, on the days when I was recording, I followed a pretty set routine. After getting up and eating breakfast, I would set off for the studio and would always stay there through the day, until about six o'clock, when it was time to come home, eat some dinner and watch some television, before going to bed. I never thought of it as work, though, and I'm not convinced that I really think of what I do now as work, either, although I'm trying to force myself to develop a better sense of compartmentalisation for my work and my personal life. But this is a funny job and it does take over your life. If you want to do well, you can't just say, 'No, it's my weekend, so I'm not going to do that.'

London was a very different sort of place from Christchurch, principally because of the scale. I loved the energy of the city. But I did miss the people back home. I didn't really know anybody in London who was not connected to making the album. I had Mum with me and, luckily, she's more like a friend than a mother. Even so, if you are a teenager and you have to spend an unnaturally large amount of your time with your parents, it can have its difficulties. Because of the nature of what I was doing, I needed to have at least one parent with me, so I guess that I'm very fortunate that Mum and I get on so well. When we go shopping, we fight over clothes; we enjoy watching the same television programmes and we like the same food, so we can hang out like friends. But, at the end of the day, she's my Mum and she's not in my age group.

At times, I did miss gossiping with my friends about clothes, or bands, or boys. I suppose it has made me quite an independent person and I enjoy having my own space. I love walking around London, just taking it all in and people-watching. I find doing chores such as going to the supermarket can give me a breather from music and performing, giving me time to think instead.

Giles Martin has a fantastic sense of humour and working in a studio with him was a very relaxed process with many laughs along the way. In fact, sometimes the laughing got in the way of recording, with many false starts, thanks to

Giles's legendary throwaway joking comments, which resulted in my being unable to contain my giggles just before I was
meant to be doing a vocal take.

Eastcote Studios, where we made half the album, were the
opposite of flashy, although they did have a real aura of
rock'n'roll about them, which I found appealing. Air
Studios, on the other hand, were very smart indeed. On the
first day I walked in, I looked up at the whiteboard on the
wall. My name was next to the sign for Studio 2. My eyes
drifted along to the other names beside mine and I was
shocked to discover that Cecilia Bartoli was in Studio 1 and
George Michael was in Studio 3. They were locked away
working and I didn't see either of them all day.

I've been back to Air Studios many times since and I often
bump into all sorts of major recording stars. Just a few days
before writing this, I saw Chris Martin from Coldplay eating
his lunch in the cafeteria. Despite its being the sort of place
where lots of different stars hang out, they keep themselves
to themselves and wander around with their people in their
own little worlds. Everyone is quite cool and, although
people acknowledge each other, they don't tend to hang
around and chat. I wonder sometimes if it would be different
if all the artists were Kiwis. We are far less reserved as a
nation than people tend to be in England.

I first met Giles's father, Sir George Martin, in the café at
Air Studios. Hanging out over lunch with him was so cool
– and there are not that many people who are in their
eighties whom you can say that about. When it was first
mentioned to me that he would be working with me on a
couple of tracks on the album, I realised quickly just how
big a thing it was by gauging the reaction of people of my
parents' generation.

He wrote 'Beat of Your Heart' and arranged 'Amazing
Grace' for me. By that stage, I was well aware of his status,
experience and background. He was a real gentleman: very

kind with his comments and generous with his time. He worked especially well with Giles. It was like having a comedy duo sitting behind the glass in the studio control room, each trying to give the other a hard time in a very good-natured way. They make an excellent team.

Sarah Class was another very important member of the *Pure* team. She added a real feminine touch to the album with her orchestral arrangements. She's very clever at making songs sound slightly lighter than a man would have done. To my mind, the song that she wrote for the album, 'Across the Universe of Time', is almost fairylike, with sparkling, glittery touches that add a magical quality to the music.

One of the highlights of making *Pure* was when it came to recording 'In Trutina' from Carl Orff's *Carmina Burana*. It was the only song that I actually recorded with the orchestra, rather than laying down my vocals after the instrumentation had been committed to tape. Each method of recording has its pros and cons, but there's something very special about standing next to an orchestra and singing with them. I find that I tend to sync my voice into the orchestral sound and the resulting track can sound more 'together'. If there are eighty or so players sitting next to you, then you realise that there will not be the opportunity to record take after take after take, so the track is often a little bit more live-sounding. Occasionally, slight idiosyncrasies in a live recording can really make a track special. That said, if you are doing a difficult piece, then it does take the pressure off if you can record separately from the orchestra. You don't have to worry about getting it right in one take to avoid paying the orchestra overtime!

I was also very excited to be singing the 'Benedictus' from *The Armed Man: A Mass for Peace* by the leading Welsh composer Karl Jenkins. He is one of the most popular and accessible contemporary classical composers around. It's a huge number and requires a big chorus. We recorded it in

Studio 1 at Air Studios, which couldn't have been more appropriate, as the whole building is a converted church, complete with stained-glass windows. There are great acoustics in Studio 1 because it has such a large area and the 'Benedictus' really filled the whole room with sound. It was the perfect setting for the piece and the atmosphere helped me a lot. It's one of the few pieces from my albums that I've never performed live and it's still something that I would love to do.

One morning, I arrived at the studios to find Giles waiting excitedly for me. He had managed to locate a Maori cultural group in London to sing on a couple of the tracks. I was a little taken aback to discover that this group existed only a few miles down the road from where I had been living, so many miles from home in New Zealand. I was very keen to have a Maori element to *Pure*, but I was not sure that we would manage to pull it off. When they came into the studio, they brought lots of New Zealand food with them to share and it became quite a party.

We also had a British choir with them in the studio at the same time. The members of the Maori cultural group were very nervous about performing in front of the choir because, although they performed professionally, they were unused to performing in the classical-music style. It was quite funny because the members of the British choir turned out to be completely in awe of the Maori cultural group and spent the whole time they were there working up the courage to ask them to perform the *haka*.

As soon as the Brits finally asked, the Maori choir did the business and it was a huge hit, really breaking down any barriers that had existed between the two groups. For me, it was so exciting to have such an authentic Kiwi atmosphere in a studio in Hampstead, North London. When the two choirs sing together on 'Pokarekare Ana', they create a magnificent sound – one of the real peaks of the whole album. Audiences outside New Zealand constantly ask me what the words to 'Pokarekare Ana' actually mean. So here is the translation.

> *Stormy are the waters*
> *Of restless Waiapu;*
> *If you cross them, girl,*
> *They will be calmed.*
> *Oh, girl,*
> *Come back to me;*
> *I could die*
> *Of love for you.*
> *I write you my letter;*
> *I send you my ring,*
> *So your people can see*
> *How troubled I am.*
> *Oh, girl,*
> *Come back to me;*
> *I could die*
> *Of love for you.*

It's the story of two lovers who are separated and is a very tragic song, although you would have been hard-pressed to realise through the buzz of excitement as we recorded it for *Pure*. It was so special to be creating this seminal New Zealand track over in London and to have a studio full of Kiwis there for support.

During the time when I was working on *Pure*, I was starting to sing in a series of live concerts around the UK with Russell Watson, who is also signed to Decca. I had already sung with him once in New Zealand in a special outdoor concert for the American television channel PBS. I opened the show for him and then we performed a duet on 'Pokarekare Ana'. It went down well with the crowd, so he invited me to join him on his tour of the UK.

This was a time when I was completely unknown, so it was a big opportunity for me. As I travelled around the UK, I began to get some sort of sense of the country as a whole, rather than just London. Russell was riding the crest of a huge number of record sales and was performing sell-out concerts in the big arenas usually reserved for pop acts, so it was a real baptism of fire for me.

The record company bought me my stage outfit: a little denim miniskirt and a sparkly top from Top Shop. It was all very girly, but it was the right look for me at that stage, although I wouldn't be seen dead wearing that sort of thing on stage now. 'You'll Never Walk Alone' was one of the songs that I performed as part of my set. It always went down well, although, just before I walked on stage in Newcastle, I had a quick lesson in English football teams and their songs from Perry Hughes, Russell's manager at the time.

'You do realise that this song is Liverpool's and you're in Newcastle – a rival?' he asked me, with a big grin on his face.

'Good to know,' I gulped, as I walked on stage. I apologised for what I was about to sing and got a huge round of applause from the very friendly (and forgiving) Newcastle crowd.

Russell's tour was the one and only occasion when Mum has appeared on stage with me at one of my professional engagements. Russell decided that he wanted to sing 'Mustang Sally' and they needed to draft in some emergency backing singers. So Mum was volunteered alongside the hair and makeup artist. It was her moment of stardom and she loved it.

I'm only glad that Dad was not there, or else he, too, might have been enrolled. Love him as I do, he really can't sing or dance. Sophie, Isaac and I are still haunted by the sight of him dressed up as Rudolph the red-nosed reindeer at the Coca-Cola Christmas in the Park concert back in

Christchurch one year when we were small. We thought that Dad would make an excellent Rudolph, but it turned out that his dancing was not quite up to scratch; and, I'm afraid to say (sorry, Dad!), his singing is not much better, either. But that is the worst thing that I can say about him – other than his singing and dancing, he's the best Dad anyone could ever have.

In June 2002, I made my debut at Carnegie Hall in New York at a concert that Russell was performing there. Once again, I performed 'Pokarekare Ana' as a duet with him, but there were technical problems halfway through my solo song. I could suddenly hear the high-pitched whistling sound of feedback. The level of the sound was starting to get bigger and bigger and I knew that at any moment it could blow into an ear-splitting screech. It's really not something that any artist would want to happen to them during their Carnegie Hall debut.

I just battled on. In a setting that prestigious, it's simply not a problem that I had expected. After all, this was not a little village hall somewhere in the country, but rather America's foremost classical-music venue. As I stood on stage, I could feel a sense of frustration welling up inside me. So much emphasis had been placed on this concert, as all the big shots from the American arm of Decca were there. A great deal of time and care had been taken over my hair, makeup and wardrobe. It was a huge deal and everything went smoothly apart from the sound – something that you would have thought they would have double- and triple-checked. People were very complimentary about my willingness to keep on going on the stage, but for me it spoiled what should have been a very special night.

A crew from the television programme *Sixty Minutes* followed my first trip to America. While we were there, they filmed me and the rest of the family taking a horse-and-cart ride around Central Park. The driver asked me why I was being filmed. I explained that I was a singer from New Zealand.

'I had Charlotte Church in my cart a few years ago,' he said. Now, Charlotte is somebody whom, although I've met her only the once, I feel I know extraordinarily well because her name came up in every single interview I gave in the first few years of my career and still comes up in every other interview I give now.

In the old days the question I was always asked was, 'Charlotte Church – do you mind the comparison?' For the record, my answer was always, 'No, it's fine. I can understand why the comparison's drawn.'

Now, the question is, 'A contemporary of yours, Charlotte Church, has gone down the pop route. Are you going to follow?' And, again, for the record, my answer is always, 'No, I'm very happy with the style of music I'm singing. I want to stay true to who I believe I am as an artist, so I'll continue working in the classical-crossover area.'

My one meeting with Charlotte was in a hotel bar, where she was sitting with her singing teacher. It was after I had appeared in Cardiff in concert with Russell Watson. After I had been on stage, Russell's manager Perry told me that Charlotte Church was in the audience. By this time, she seemed like the most famous person in the world to me, as her name was trotted out by every journalist I ever talked to, the world over.

We finally met at the St David's Hotel later that evening. I was sitting with Mum and a few of the musicians and I breathed in sharply when I saw her in the doorway. I nudged Mum and whispered, 'Charlotte Church's just come in.' I was suddenly very nervous of meeting this girl, who was only a year older than I was. Afterwards, I turned to Mum and said, 'How cool, getting to meet her!'

We were introduced and I talked to her very briefly, but she was constantly sending text messages on her mobile phone. Apparently, her boyfriend was waiting for her in the car outside, so she didn't really want to be doing the whole meet-'n'-greet thing. She was wearing a cute cap and she looked very starry as she walked into the bar. Everyone turned to look at her and I felt like a country bumpkin in comparison. It didn't worry me and it was not a big deal, although I did silently wish that I could look that stylish.

'Oh, yes, great concert. You're doing very well. Congratulations,' she said.

'It's lovely to be meeting you,' I replied. 'Congratulations on your success too.'

Our conversation was very polite – not tense at all, but just polite. Looking back, I guess it should have been more tense than it was because we were very much seen as competitors in the same market at the time. Now, we are a million miles apart in what we do.

Another big star whom I nearly met was Victoria Beckham, but she makes it into this book only because I said 'no' to her. Sorry, Victoria. Her parents came to the concert that Russell and I gave at Wembley Stadium. While I was performing, her parents held up their mobile phone so that she could hear how I sounded. I was then invited to sing at one of the Beckhams' exclusive showbiz parties. To the shock of many of my friends, I turned them down.

To be honest with you, I would love to have gone along, but I was committed to performing in a series of concerts back in New Zealand, and in one of them my sister Sophie was due to perform with me. She was all psyched up for it and was really looking forward to the experience. I couldn't possibly let her down. I was also worried about cancelling the show and disappointing my fans. It obviously was not an easy decision to make, but I do believe that once an artist has made a commitment to do something, and their fans have paid out their cash for tickets and are eagerly awaiting the show date, the artist should do everything possible to honour the commitment to their fans. And that means sometimes having to say no to other fantastic invitations that come along on the way. No performer should ever take their fans for granted.

By now, I was living a fairly nomadic existence, flying back and forth to New Zealand. We moved into a flat in the bustling Covent Garden area of London, which became our European base. I had been quite homesick for New Zealand on my first trip and, although I do still miss my friends and family when I'm away for a long period, I'm more used to it these days. Throughout the period that I was making *Pure*, I was attempting to carry on with my schooling at Burnside High School, although my absences were not looking too good on the attendance register.

When I was there, I did well, particularly in maths and science, and I was reasonably good at English. If I'm being honest, I would have to say that by this stage, with so much happening to me in terms of my music career, my heart was not really in school. As I neared the end of my high school years, I felt that even if my marks were a little on the low side, it wouldn't matter, since I didn't need bits of paper to make it as a singer. Mum and Dad took a slightly more pragmatic view and were keen for me to keep up with my schoolwork. They, along with my lawyer, did some negoti-ating with the record company and organised a tutor for me while I was in London, although this still was not ideal, since he didn't travel with me, so I could have lessons only on my days off from recording. I suppose that my school-work did come second to my music. Put it this way: I don't ever remember doing homework sitting at the back of a recording studio. I probably should have been keeping up with schoolwork on a daily basis, but, instead, everything had to be squeezed into the occasional day off.

I ended up taking the British GCSE exams a year later because, the year that I was due to take the New Zealand School Certificate, a new system had been introduced, which made it very difficult for teachers to give me work that they had prepared in advance. There was also a good deal of internal assessment, with the aim of taking pressure off the students by assessing coursework through the year and making the final exam only part of the overall mark. The problem for me was that, because I was constantly travelling, I missed each of these assessment dates. That meant that my potential grades at the end of the year were gradually being eroded away. I did manage to sit the end-of-year exams and my grades were good, but I could have done so much better had I been there throughout the year – hence the need for me to do GCSEs when I was in the UK.

I've not carried on with any formal further education after that, but I honestly don't feel that I've missed out. Nobody ever asks me about exams or grades these days, although there seems to be a general assumption that I finished my high school years up to NCEA Level 3 in New Zealand, or A-levels in the UK.

Sure, there are times when I wish that I had continued my German and French. They would have actually been useful for me as I travel around, but I think my time is much better spent on my singing career. It's not too late either. I've just bought myself an Italian language course, which I'm studying at home. There's always time to keep on learning. I'm a firm believer that, for people with enquiring minds, learning never stops – and it does not have to be formal, either. I'm planning to keep on working on my Italian, because it will be useful for my singing, particularly since many of my favourite arias come from Italian operas. At the moment, I work on the basis of reading a translation of a song and then knowing how the words sound, rather than being able to translate it directly myself. I've picked up a little of the language through singing it, but, if I went to Italy, I would be completely stuck.

After I had finished recording *Pure*, Giles and his team worked on making the album ready for presentation to the record-company bosses. One particular song that we had recorded was to prove to be a big sticking point for everyone concerned. I fell in love with 'Wuthering Heights' after Mum played me the original Kate Bush version back home in Christchurch. We were working through the family's record collection looking for potential songs for me to record and she put the disc on the turntable in the living room. Out came the utterly unique sound of Kate Bush.

'What on earth is this?' I asked her incredulously. I really didn't know whether I liked it or not, but it was very different from anything I had heard before. It's one of those songs that really grow on you, and I listened to it again and again, letting it whirr over in my mind. Soon, I was dancing around the house to it. I couldn't get the song out of my head.

'I *have* to record this song,' I said to Mum. And that is exactly what I did with Giles when we came to work together on the album. The Decca bosses had other ideas, though, when they heard the album. The ominous message came back: 'We just don't think that "Wuthering Heights" fits.'

I was not happy and I was not backing down.

There were an inordinate number of phone calls and then suddenly it came to the big meeting. It had turned into a big deal and I was called into the Universal building, where all of the senior executives had turned out. There were a lot of them there, so it was just as well that I had brought along my whole family as my support crew. It was quite an intimidating environment for a fifteen-year-old girl to find herself in, but, strangely enough, I felt quietly confident.

I was very firm with myself ahead of the meeting: 'Hayley, you're not to back down,' I instructed myself. 'Don't be nice. You believe in this song, so go for it.' I knew that I was resolute on this. There was nothing they could do to slay me.

They soon got the message when I started crying. The meeting had dragged on with the bosses going on and on about it, but I was quietly sure of my opinion. I was not cynically turning on the tears. At the time, I didn't realise they would help me, but, of course, large groups of middle-aged blokes always struggle to cope with a girl bursting into tears. The waterworks worked.

'I think that this meeting has come to an end, so we'll think about it and then we'll get back to you,' I was told. Later, Costa Pilavachi called me up.

'We now know that you feel really strongly about this song,' he said. 'And, if you feel this strongly about it, we don't feel that we're in any position to stand in your way. One thing I always say is that the artist is always right.' As ever, Costa had been very diplomatic and very sweet. He always instinctively knew how to say the right thing at the right time. So 'Wuthering Heights' stayed on the album.

Pure was first released in New Zealand in July 2003 with the UK release coming a couple of months later. Back home, I toured around all the radio stations accompanied by the guitarist Kurt Shanks. This allowed me to give impromptu performances of the songs, which always went down a treat. The presenters seemed genuinely surprised to discover an artist who was prepared to sing the songs from her album on demand and without the safety net of the recording studio's electronic wizardry. One of the upsides of the promotion phase of a record's life is that all the expenses are paid for by the record company, so you tend to be well looked after. The artist's meals are paid for and you are put up in nice hotels. Each territory around the world vies to look after you the best – probably just to make sure that you actually come back again next time.

One of the more challenging parts of doing promotion is the relentless round of interviews, which can become very monotonous. Sometimes, I have to sit in a hotel room for a whole day, which has been divided into ten-minute blocks, one for each different journalist. That is a tough call when they come in through the door one after another. I often find myself struggling to remember what I've said to the other journalists who have already interviewed me and whether I'm repeating myself or not.

Sometimes I try to change my answers, just to keep myself alert. I try to think about each question in a new light, rather than just giving the same answer over and over again, because, if you repeat the same reply all the time, it can come to sound too rehearsed. The risk of attempting to vary each answer is that it does not come out right because I'm trying to avoid saying what I would usually say, when it would be much easier to have just given a tried and tested answer. The best interviews are those that seem more like conversations, as opposed to my being thrown a series of questions in the order that they are written on the interviewer's notepad.

One of my favourite interviews happened in Japan. Rather than the normal session about how I came to have an album deal, what my school friends thought of my having an album and the ubiquitous Charlotte Church question, all I had to do was give my verdict on a series of different Japanese sweets and cakes. It was a bit different and didn't require me to do too much thinking; it was more a workout for my taste buds than anything else.

I also enjoy it when I'm asked random questions, usually at the end of an interview after all the normal stuff. This particularly happens on local radio stations, where the presenter asks me a series of completely unpredictable questions, such as whether I prefer fish and chips or curry. (It's fish and chips, by the way – although Steve, my manager, is forever trying to convert me to curry.)

Pure went straight to the top of the charts in New Zealand. At that stage, we were not to know that it would go on to become the country's biggest-selling album ever by a local artist. As I read that sentence back, it still sounds like the stuff of dreams to me and I can't quite believe it, even now. There certainly was no time to take it in back in 2003, because no sooner had I finished promoting the album at home than I jumped back on a plane to London to work on the UK launch. In terms of sales, if we got it right, this would be the big one.

Just before that album's release in the UK, I performed at Bryn Terfel's Faenol Festival in North Wales. This is an annual event, organised by Bryn, near to his home. As it turned out, Faenol was one of the most significant events in my career, although at the time I had no idea just how important it would prove to be. It was my first introduction to Wales and, at this stage, I was still pretty much unknown in the UK. I did some interviews in a magnificent part of North Wales. We stayed in a beautiful hotel that was surrounded by grassy hills. The contrast with London and city life was wonderful; it felt as though I had been transported to a picturesque, tranquil wilderness, filled with some of the most friendly people I've ever met.

When I walked on stage, I was blown away by the huge response from the audience – and this was a group of people who didn't know me at all. The people were so lovely and the warmth of the welcome was very genuine, not least from Bryn Terfel himself. He is an incredibly nice man and is one of the greatest singers I've ever had the privilege to hear.

What amazed me the most was how at one moment he could be standing at the side of the stage in fits of laughter at someone's joke, and then, within two seconds, walk on stage and sing magnificently in full character. I've never seen anyone to whom singing comes so easily. As I've got to know him better over the years since, I've warmed to his larger-than-life personality even more. He always takes time to ask about my family whenever I see him and I always ask him about his home in Wales.

One of the highlights of the day was rehearsing with Bryn and José Carreras in a caravan that was parked around the back of the temporary stage that had been put up specifically for the festival. They made it great fun and there was probably more laughing than singing, if I'm totally honest. Walking out on stage with them later that evening was a magical moment. It sealed a very special relationship that I've enjoyed with the people of Wales ever since. I was thrilled to be invited to sing at the International Eisteddfod in the summer of 2007. I always love going back there to perform.

The other significant event about Faenol was that it was the moment that I first met the man who was to become my manager, Steve Abbott. Years after the event Steve (or Abbo, as he's known to his friends) confessed that he had been really nervous about meeting me. So much so, that he had been out and bought a whole lot of new shirts and a suit, thinking that, if he was going to be working in the classical-music world, he had better make himself look respectable. When I met him, I had no idea that he had made such an effort, so, when I was told, I was quite chuffed.

Steve had been brought to Faenol by a couple of the record-company people. I needed a full-time manager, because it was becoming too big a job for Mum and Dad to do on their own. Things didn't go completely in Steve's favour on the day. He had an umbrella sticking out from his bag and, as he walked along the side of the catering marquee, it knocked all the wineglasses off a table on to the floor in one fell swoop. Not only was he trying to impress us, but he also wanted to leave a good impression in the minds of the record-company people. He must have wanted the earth to swallow him up.

Steve is not your typical manager. He amuses me enormously. He's a very hands-on manager and he doesn't just sit on his own in his office. Instead, he likes to get out on the road, as we found out shortly after Faenol when I sang at a series of concerts with Aled Jones. Steve used to pick me and Mum up at our flat, having stopped off at a health-food shop to buy vegetable pasties and muesli bars to fortify us on the journey. We would then hit the road with Steve at the wheel of a car that was definitely not at limousine standards of luxury!

He is very down to earth and that is one of the reasons we work so well together. He became part of the family; it was a big trust thing for Mum and Dad to hand over their daughter to a manager, but he's always worked very closely with them. He continued to consult with them and has had to work more closely with my family than other managers might have had to do, because I was so young. I suppose he's like an uncle to me.

As things have grown, so has the team at Steve's company, Bedlam Management. First, he worked with Giselle Allier, who is now a showbiz lawyer. She's a very sweet and caring personality and we developed a very close relationship. When she left to practise law full-time, Kathryn Nash took over. Along with Steve, she's now my co-manager and, whereas Steve takes on an avuncular role, Kathryn is like a big sister to me. The other two members of the Bedlam team are Nicola Goodall, who looks after the diaries and ensures that everything runs smoothly behind the scenes, and Erica Sprigge, who has recently joined to run the concert agency part of Bedlam's activities.

I'm also very lucky to have been working, from the start of my time in the UK, with Dickon Stainer and Mark Wilkinson, the bosses of the UK arm of Universal, which is called Universal Classics and Jazz, or UCJ for short. Although I'm signed to Decca, Dickon and Mark are responsible for selling and marketing my albums in the UK. They have always been incredibly supportive of what I do and, between them, they masterminded the most amazing campaign to launch *Pure*.

At the end of the first day's sales, we were all shocked to discover just how effective Dickon and Mark had been, with the album sitting at number twelve in the pop charts. That meant that there was a very real chance that it could take the record for the best-selling first-week sales by a debut artist in the UK classical charts. The UCJ team flicked back through the history books and discovered that the record was held by none other than my old friend, Charlotte Church. I really wanted to wrestle the title from her grip.

I was aware that first-week sales were particularly important in the British marketplace, because, if you don't do well, then the record company and retailers quickly lose interest and you find yourself being dropped by the important shops. It's different in the USA, where the expectation is that you will gradually work your way up the charts.

Most of the interviews had been done in the run-up to the launch of the album, so my schedule was quieter in the week of the actual launch than it had been for weeks beforehand. On the Saturday of that first week, the final day that would make any difference to the initial sales, I was sitting in my flat twiddling my thumbs.

'I need to be doing something. I know it's going to be tight,' I said to Dad. 'I'd hate it to be just a few album sales that's the difference between my getting the first-week sales record and not.'

So, I hatched a plan to visit as many big record stores as I possibly could in central London and to offer to sign CDs, which I had been asked to do in the past on organised record-store visits. I travelled around to each of them on my own on the Tube. When I first walked into HMV in Covent Garden, I was halfway around the world from home and it gave me an incredible buzz to see a whole column of my albums facing me. Wow! This is so cool! I thought silently to myself. I stood there watching people pick them up. I tried mentally to send them messages saying, 'Buy it! Buy it! Buy it!'

If I discovered a store where the CD was not prominent enough, I would surreptitiously start moving CDs around on the shelves. By the time I had finished, it would sometimes remarkably be sitting at numbers one, two, three and four in the charts. Looking back on it now, I'm amazed that I didn't have a troop of store detectives following my every move. It was a little like a military operation and, once I had eyeballed the shelves, my next tactic was to sidle up to the counter and engage the shop assistant in conversation.

'I just happened to be passing the store,' I would say, my eyes wide with innocence. 'You've got some copies of my new album on the shelves over there and I wondered if you'd like me to sign some of them for you.'

The final part of the operation was for me to suggest that they play the album on the in-store PA system. When I had achieved all three of these objectives, I would move on to my next target, a few blocks down the road, leaving a bemused shop assistant in my wake. It was quite an effective campaign, but I want to assure you that it's something that I've never done since – and I don't have any intention of doing again in the future!

Over the preceding few months, I had been working with Lisa Davies, who handled the booking of my television and radio interviews, as she does for a whole range of different classical artists. The UK charts are published on Sunday lunchtimes and I was sitting with Dad in her garden when the call came through. She turned to me and said, 'You're number one in the classical charts and number eight in the pop charts – and you've broken the record.'

I was thrilled and we all drank a glass of champagne – something that I wouldn't usually have done at the time, but, if you can't have a glass of champagne when you've just broken the record for best-selling first week by a debut artist in the UK classical charts, then when *can* you?

We had seen the midweek charts, which are circulated around the record companies but not released to the public, and things had looked good. But I had been scared that the sales for my album might drop off at the weekend. I had been told that my pop-music competitors tended to do better at the end of the week because they had promotion from the television shows such as *Top of the Pops* and *CD:UK*, so I was concerned that I might be eclipsed by a pop act. I so much wanted the album to be successful because of all the hard work that everyone had put into it. This was crunch time.

For a moment, I thought that the pressure would be off after the strong first week's performance, but in fact it increased dramatically. I had been so focused on doing everything I could for it to be a good first week. Then I realised that I would have to redouble my efforts to ensure that *Pure* sustained its success. I carried on like a hamster in a wheel, going round and round doing promotional interviews and appearances. Whenever I had a day off, I would get stressed that I should be doing something. I was not happy to sit still and just take time out. Instead, I was willing to do anything for the album's success. I realise now that it makes me sound desperate, but in reality I was just extremely determined.

The international success spurred on sales of *Pure* in New Zealand. It really started to take off when my fellow Kiwis heard how well it was doing abroad, with huge coverage in the New Zealand media. In the end, *Pure* went eighteen-times platinum back home.

It's funny, but sometimes we need someone else to give the nod of approval before we Kiwis accept something as cool. It can be quite hard for local bands to break, unless they have had an element of international success. I think we sometimes look abroad for a stamp of approval on our home-grown talent, which can occasionally be taken for granted.

CHAPTER 8
SINGING FOR MY SUPPER

After the success of *Pure* in the UK, I made brief visits to countries all over the world to promote the album. It was late in 2003, just after Dad and I had returned to our flat in London's Covent Garden. That same day, Dad took a call from Steve Abbott. I could hear only Dad's end of the conversation, but I could tell that he was excited about whatever it was that they had been talking about. When he put the phone down, he seemed almost reluctant to pass on the message, because he knew the effect it would have on me.

'Andrew Lloyd Webber wants to meet with you. You have an audition with him,' he said with a broad grin on his face. 'And the audition's tomorrow'.

It was this last part that worried Dad. He knew that I was already exhausted after a particularly arduous trip to Japan and, as we had only just arrived back in London, the jetlag was still to kick in.

'This is fantastic,' I said, hugging Dad. 'But couldn't he have given me a week's notice?'

Let me say right now that absolutely nobody is a bigger fan of Lord Lloyd-Webber's music than I am. From my very earliest days I've sung his songs. His music speaks volumes to me and even my earliest demo CD featured some of it. Even though it felt like an impossibility that I would be ready to audition for him in the morning, I knew that it was something that I had to do. That night, I had trouble sleeping, since not only was I full of nerves, I was also completely jetlagged. My mind was buzzing with questions about the following day. What would I be auditioning for? Would I manage to perform to the best of my ability? What should I sing? And what would happen if Andrew Lloyd Webber didn't like what he heard?

The offices of his company, the Really Useful Group, were just around the corner from our flat in Covent Garden. As we headed towards the building's front door, I knew that I really wanted to wow him with my singing. I was even more excited when Steve told Dad and me that I was auditioning for something that was top-secret. He didn't have a clue what it might be for, but the people from the Really Useful Group had told him that it was very urgent that Lord Lloyd-Webber (as he has been since 1997) see me on this particular day, although they were very fuzzy in the details of why speed was so necessary.

The offices struck me as being very smart. I was shown through into the wooden-floored music room where a grand piano was positioned in the corner. Dad and Steve waited outside in an office area. There was no sign of Andrew Lloyd Webber. Instead, I was greeted by his musical director. I was beginning to feel even more nervous and confused because at that time I had no idea who this man was.

'Let's sing through this piece here, then,' he said, passing me some music that I had never seen before: a new duet from the musical *The Woman in White* called 'I Believe My Heart'.

I started to sing and, as I did so, all sorts of thoughts rushed through my mind. I was worried that the piece might be too high, too low, too this, too that – but it suited my voice well. I knew that I needed to look competent in front of Andrew Lloyd Webber and, because the piece was completely new to me, I had to read the music by sight as we went along. Andrew's colleague just played the accompaniment and let me carry the tune all by myself.

I thanked my lucky stars that Mum and Dad had encouraged me to learn the violin and piano, since this was exactly the sort of occasion when all of those hours of practice came in handy. It's funny how you do some things in life and then give them up, but you still utilise the skills that you have learned along the way.

I was feeling quietly confident that I was managing to hit the notes and then I heard this creak behind me and I just knew that it was Andrew Lloyd Webber.

Oh boy, oh boy! I thought to myself. I could see a high note coming. 'Hayley, you'd better get that note!' I told myself, all the time singing my way towards it. 'I've done it! I got the note!'

The pianist stopped playing and then Andrew Lloyd Webber shook my hand and introduced himself, although he needed to make absolutely no introduction to me, his biggest fan. He came across as quite a quiet and reserved man. He stood listening to me sing some more with his right-hand man accompanying me on piano.

'Well, everything they say about you is true,' he said. I smiled, silently hoping that whoever 'they' were had said good things about me. Then he decided that he wanted to sit down at the piano to take over playing. He complimented me on my voice and I began to feel slightly more relaxed as I seemed to have passed the test so far – although, since he didn't say too much, I was still not entirely certain where I stood.

'Have you sung much of my music?' he asked.

'Oh, yes, since I was very small,' I replied.

'What other songs of mine do you know?'

I suggested 'Wishing You Were Somehow Here Again' and immediately regretted it. A wave of panic swept through me. Would I remember all the words? After all, it had been a long time since I had sung the song. He started playing and it was incredible. I managed to remember the words, thank goodness. It was just amazing having him at the piano and suddenly the song became so much more meaningful to me for some reason. I could tell that he was listening carefully and, at one point, he became quite teary-eyed, although I never knew why.

'Beautiful,' he said. 'You can certainly sing.' He may not have said much, but what he did say was important to me. Those few positive words were very meaningful. Here I was, singing in front of one of my all-time musical heroes. I couldn't quite believe that it was happening to me.

'What about "Pie Jesu"?' he asked. I told him that this was among the songs of his that I performed most often. I sang it all the way through.

It was time to leave, and, as I said goodbye to Lord Lloyd-Webber, I got the idea that I had been given the job, although I still didn't know what the job was. I had already decided that I would do it, whatever it was, simply because Andrew Lloyd Webber was involved.

Shortly afterwards, Steve was told, in the utmost secrecy that I would be performing for the Queen, President George

W Bush and Prime Minister Tony Blair, after a dinner to be held at the American Ambassador's residence in Hyde Park. We knew that we had to keep my part in the concert completely quiet, so we developed our own code for talking about the event, describing it as 'the Barbecue', taking the letters BBQ from the words Blair, Bush and Queen. It meant that we could discuss the finer details of what was going on, without anybody else actually knowing what we were talking about.

The big day was during the following week and I spent the morning rehearsing at the Really Useful Group offices. My fellow performers included two singers from Andrew Lloyd Webber's musical *Bombay Dreams*, who were going to sing 'How Many Stars'; an Irish singer, Shonagh Daly; and Kevin McKidd, with whom I was duetting on 'I Believe My Heart'. I also had a solo performance of 'Pie Jesu'.

I had spent a few days considering what I should wear for such an auspicious occasion and, in the end, I chose a dress designed by Jenny Packham. She's a British designer whom I really like. She's become quite a big name recently. Her dresses were ideal for me, since they struck a perfect balance between being young and being classy. My choice for the 'Barbecue' was a lemon-coloured creation, with coloured beaded butterflies on it.

For security reasons, only Lord Lloyd-Webber, the musical director and the artists were allowed to travel to the American Ambassador's residence. I left Steve and Dad waiting in Covent Garden. We all piled into a big black van. It felt as if we were on some sort of secret mission, since we had secret-service guys with us talking into their cuffs. We felt very special, although everyone admitted that their levels of nervousness were beginning to outweigh the general air of excitement.

When we arrived at the gates, we drove through as many as six different checkpoints, with the van being checked outside and inside, and each of the individuals being examined closely. Eventually we arrived at the inner gates to the house, where we were checked once again.

Of course, I had tons of luggage with me, as usual. I had wanted to be prepared, so I had packed my makeup, my hair stuff, a spare dress, spare shoes, a book to read and my laptop. It had not seemed an unreasonable amount when I had stuffed it all into my bag that morning, although now, as everyone else was forced to wait for the security guys to go through each item in detail, I realised that perhaps I might have travelled a little lighter.

After what seemed like an eternity, we were ushered into a small side room to get ourselves ready. I was really nervous by now. Along with the Queen, George W Bush and Tony Blair were Prince Philip, Prince Charles, Condoleezza Rice and Colin Powell, as well as a host of other British and American dignitaries. It was probably the most powerful collection of people that I would ever perform in front of in my life. But it was not they who worried me one little bit. There was only one person whose presence was making me nervous.

It was Andrew Lloyd Webber. You see, I was singing his songs and the last thing I wanted to do was to mess them up. I really wanted him to be impressed by me as a singer and I was far less worried about what George W Bush or Tony Blair thought. I reckoned that they would have other things on their minds and wouldn't be paying too much attention to the music. Andrew, on the other hand, would be listening to every note and would know instantly if anything went wrong.

My turn eventually came to walk in through the doors to perform in front of the dinner guests. There were around fifty people sitting there and the room was not really big enough to hold them all when you factor a piano and performers into the equation, so I found myself almost brushing up against one of the guests. I was quaking in my shoes and it was quite possibly the most nervous I've ever felt before or since. The great man was there throughout, right in front of me, just to the left. I scanned the room, trying to remain focused on singing, but it's impossible to be so in such a small space and not to notice the Queen, Prince Philip and Prince Charles.

I was trying my hardest to focus on the back wall, but it was very strange having all of these familiar faces staring back from such a close proximity. President Bush was leaning back on his chair looking relaxed. He is a very charismatic man with a big presence. He spent the whole time looking appreciative with a smile on his face.

I was worried about singing 'Pie Jesu', because it's a tough song with some pretty big vocal jumps in it. The key thing is not to form a complex about singing difficult songs. Once I've stumbled over a particular line, that stays with me for ever and I become paranoid about the song in question. But 'Pie Jesu' went fantastically for me on the night.

After everyone had sung their solo pieces and their duets, we all sang 'No Matter What', which I had never previously realised was an Andrew Lloyd Webber song. It first came on to my musical radar when it was performed by the boy band, Boyzone. Mum will probably kill me for writing this, but she was a particularly big fan of theirs at the height of their fame.

Afterwards, we waited in a line to meet each of the dignitaries. I didn't know at the time that Condoleezza Rice was a highly proficient piano player. Had I done so, I would have worried even more, because performing in front of anyone who I know has a musical ear makes me nervous. We all had our picture taken with President Bush; he had his arm around me. He was very warm and appreciative to everyone. At the end he turned to me and said, 'Your performance really capped off the evening. Well done – you have a great voice.'

When Prince Charles came by, I reminded him that he had visited my primary school back home in Christchurch when I was six. 'Oh, really, did I?' he said, with a very genial smile. I reassured him that it was OK if he couldn't remember.

Funnily enough, I had met the Queen three times in a fairly short period. I had already sung for her at the Royal Variety Show in Edinburgh, where I had performed a medley of 'Pokarekare Ana' (with Maori dancers) and 'Amazing Grace' (with bagpipes). Later in the week, I performed at the Remembrance Day concert at the Royal Albert Hall in London.

In the line-up afterwards, she asked me, 'Didn't I see you earlier on this week?'

'Yes, ma'am,' I replied. 'And I'm going to be singing for you again in a few days' time.

At this point, I've a confession to make – something that I've never revealed before in any interview about this particular evening at the American Ambassador's place. I was determined to have a memento of the occasion and you will understand that I'm not entirely sure how a serviette embroidered with the little American Embassy symbol somehow came home with me in my bag. It's probably the naughtiest thing that I've ever done. Well, almost! When I visited the White House four years later, I was careful to ensure that I didn't repeat my misdemeanour. On this occasion, two sachets of sugar emblazoned with the presidential seal managed to find their way into my bag – one contained brown sugar and the other white. Can you believe they have their own sugar sachets?

As we got ready to leave the Hyde Park, I was still more concerned about what Andrew Lloyd Weber thought of my performance than about any of the other high-flying guests. I had not spoken to him at this stage and I was still holding my breath when we were whisked off to dinner at the Wolsey, one of London's smartest restaurants. Dad and

Steve met me at the door with a television crew from New Zealand who interviewed me about the evening. Dinner was all a bit of a blur for me. It was such an event and I was pretty relieved when it was all over. We were very well looked after in the restaurant, sitting at a table that overlooked the other diners – without question, the best seats in the place.

At the very end of the meal, Andrew Lloyd Webber came up to me and congratulated me on my performance. 'In fact, I'm going to write a song for you,' he said.

'Wow! Oh my gosh!' was all that I could stammer as a reply.

When we arrived back at the flat, I phoned Mum in New Zealand to tell her about one of the most remarkable evenings of my life. I was on a major high with adrenalin pumping through me, as often happens after I've given a good performance at a big concert. When this happens, it's very fulfilling because I feel that I've made a connection with the audience. It feels as if I've done a good day's work.

As I lay in bed that night, I had trouble sleeping. The events of the preceding few hours were still buzzing through my mind. It had not just been a good day's work: it had been an *extraordinarily* good day's work. And it had been made all the more special because I had gained the approval of Andrew Lloyd Webber, something that had been so important to me for so long.

CHAPTER 9
ODYSSEY

The perceived wisdom in the music industry is that one of the toughest things for any artist who has had a successful debut album is to create a successful follow-up album. I know that *Pure* was in fact my third professional album, but it was my first for Decca, so that meant that, as far as everyone was concerned, my next album would be considered the follow-up.

Initially, I found the process exciting because I was itching to get back into the recording studio to create something new, since it had been well over eighteen months since I had recorded *Pure.* One of the drawbacks about having an album that does well in a number of different territories around the world is that the artist has to spend a long time promoting that album, rather than getting on and making a new one.

By this stage, I felt that I had moved up from the level I was at when I recorded *Pure* and I was excited about having the opportunity to prove myself in the studio once again. I had quite a few different ideas for the album and I wanted people to hear my new work and to feel that I had evolved both in terms of my technical ability as a singer and also in terms of my general presence as a performer.

I'm very lucky that my voice is quite versatile and my musical tastes are quite varied. This does throw up some challenges, though, and, when it came to making my second album for Decca, I found it hard to know what musical direction I should be travelling in. That can make the process of creating an album quite a struggle. At that stage, I was still relatively young and I didn't want to restrict myself by finding that I had been put into a box by the music industry as the sort of artist who could do only this, or could never do that. I figured that further down the track I could make some more tightly themed albums.

At the same time, I wanted my new album to sound complete. This was a tricky set of decisions for me and, looking back, I probably should have stuck to my guns a lot more, instead of being pulled in lots of different directions by various record companies around the world, each of whom wanted something slightly different for their particular market. I listened to the opinions of a lot of people about which songs I should be doing. That said, though, in no way do I regard the album as a mistake. If everything you do as an artist is perfect, then you will never grow. This new album was an accurate snapshot of me as a performer at the beginning of 2005.

It's hard enough to choose songs for an album, but another conundrum that any artist has to consider very carefully is the question of what to call an album. I settled on *Odyssey* because, at the outset, I wanted to take the listener on a journey through different countries and through different moods. I, myself, had been on a massive journey all of my own – both literally, in terms of how far I had travelled from home, and also as a singer and a person. I wanted to share some sort of sense of that with the listeners.

Emotionally, my journey had also been something of a roller-coaster ride. By now, I was used to coming off stage on a huge high and having people applauding me. Meeting the fans after the concerts was always a buzz and I was always in great spirits after each concert. Then, I would find myself back in a hotel room, not just in a strange city, but often in a strange country. I would start to miss everyone and would feel isolated. Some days I was exhausted and other days I was full of energy. I've come to realise now that this epitomises the life of an international singer, but when I came to make *Odyssey*, everything had been happening so fast that I'm not sure that I had actually had time to sit down and rationalise this.

I was still discovering and experimenting with lots of different styles of music. I had grown up listening to classical music and, as a child, I had both played and sung some of the better-known parts of the repertoire. But I really didn't know nearly as much about it as I wanted to and I was enjoying discovering new works by people I had never come across before. I was also discovering aspects of folk and pop music that I had never previously encountered. In the period between *Pure* and *Odyssey*, I spent a lot of my time travelling and so had the opportunity to listen to piles of great albums. I love music, full stop. But it was all getting kind of confusing because there were so many different styles that I found exciting and appealing.

When I was growing up back in New Zealand, my musical influences had included the likes of Andrea Bocelli, Kathleen Battle, Vanessa Carlton, Alicia Keyes, Celine Dion, the boy band BackStreet Boys, the all-girl group B*witched and the Norwegian classical-crossover group Secret Garden. I even enjoyed contemporary classical compilation albums such as my favourite, panpipe-heavy *Moods* album, which I listened to while I was studying. The Spice Girls were another of my big loves. One afternoon at home, my next-door neighbours, Emma and Nicola Ritchie, joined Sophie and me in dressing up in denim shorts and little tops so that we could put on a Spice Girls concert. We knew all the words to the songs, although we made up our own moves. I was always Sporty Spice because I looked the most like her with my brown hair, but secretly I always wanted to be Baby Spice – that was always Sophie because she had blonde hair. I guess we were all into the idea of 'girl power', and the Spice Girls were, to an extent, all strong female role models for us young girls. Their ethos centred on the things that girls could achieve. They also recorded the most amazingly catchy songs. So, my CD collection was a pretty eclectic mix. I'm not sure that many other twelve-year-olds in Christchurch had a Spice Girls CD and an album by the soprano Kathleen Battle sitting side by side on a shelf in their bedrooms.

Back then, I was very much into the contemporary pop music of the day. Now, I'm much more interested in the quality of great songwriting, and so I listen to the likes of Stevie Wonder, the Carpenters and ABBA. I'm really enjoying listening to great songs, and the lyrical content of each track I hear is particularly important to me. When I was younger, I would tune into the music rather than the lyrics. Most of the time, the words didn't really mean anything to me because they were about things that I couldn't really relate to, such as the ups and downs of romantic relationships.

For me, Benny Andersson and Björn Ulvaeus, the two men behind Abba, rank as among the best songwriters of all time. They wrote amazing songs, which are still technically brilliant when you deconstruct them. When I started to write my own songs, I would write everything in minor keys. I'm not quite sure why, but I suppose that I must have felt that my music would be more sophisticated if they had a minor sound to them. But then, when I started looking at Abba songs, I realised that they tend to be in major keys. They have very simple, but highly effective, chord patterns and the overall sound is very optimistic. They are still so successful today because they knew how to write songs that people want to listen to.

Because my first album had sold so many copies, songwriters were keen for me to record their music on the follow-up. When you become established, people even begin to write songs with you in mind and send them to you unsolicited. I wanted to sing songs that gave me the chance to say something meaningful, but many of the writers who sent me material had an image of this young girl in their mind. I can imagine the process that they went through.

'What's she going to want to sing about?' they would ask themselves. 'Well, she's still young, so let's make her sing about dolphins and fairies and magical things, instead of anything with real substance.'

One songwriter who didn't do this was Jeff Franzel. I was very drawn to one of his tracks called 'Never Saw Blue', which was very easy on the ear and was in the same vein as 'Who Painted the Moon Black?' from *Pure*. It had quite a pop sound to it, but I felt that this could be balanced by other tracks on the album. Jeff came to the studio and played it to the team working on the new album and everyone seemed to love it.

'Cool,' I said. 'That's one song down for the album.' Basically, this was how things developed from there onwards, one song at a time.

At the classical end of the spectrum, I felt that I was ready to record some bigger opera pieces such as 'Lascia Ch'io Piangia', Caccini's 'Ave Maria' and 'O Mio Babbino Caro'. These sat very comfortably alongside 'Never Saw Blue' in terms of maintaining the variety of different types of music that had worked so well on *Pure*. I was also determined to record 'Quanta Qualia', a track by the English contemporary classical composer Patrick Hawes, which I felt was an incredibly atmospheric piece.

Working in the studio is an expensive business, so I tend not actually to record anything until I'm absolutely sure that I like it. I try to filter out as many tracks as possible, generally based on the lyrics and the piano part sent by each of the prospective writers. Usually, I judge any potential track by the way that I feel on my first listen to it. Lyrics are so important to me that, if someone has written a song and the words are too naff, I'll immediately switch off to the track, no matter how strong the melody may be.

As I flew home on the plane to New Zealand that Christmas, I listened to dozens of potential songs and, while I was there, I often received CDs in the post from the A&R boss at Decca, Jacky Schroer. It's her job to help work with artists to develop the repertoire on their albums. She flagged up particular songs and then I would respond with a yes or a no. The songs that I immediately declined were those that I simply didn't like or those that didn't suit my voice. I was really open to as many different ideas as possible, although I seemed to be dogged by dozens of very cheesy offerings.

At home, I sat in my bedroom, blasting out CDs on the stereo that I had won in one of the Talent Quest competitions. I wanted to make sure that I chose songs that grabbed me on the first listen, as there's always a danger of becoming familiar with a song and then finding yourself enjoying it only because you know it so well. It's important that a song should not burn out quickly in listeners' affections once they have heard it a few times, but the most significant thing has to be the way that a great song hooks someone in on the very first listen.

I was keen to include some of my own songs for *Odyssey*, and I'd been writing on my own, but I was not really at the stage where I was comfortable sharing my creations with all these people and opening myself to criticism. I worked on many of the arrangements on the album, which was a great experience, and I also co-wrote my first track, called 'What You Never Know (Won't Hurt You)', with a great song-writer called Stephan Moccio. I wanted to make sure that the track was as good as I hoped it was. So, while I was in New Zealand, I took my Walkman with me to a rock festival called Big Day Out, which sees visits from bands all over the world. I was sitting at a table with a friend from home called Anita Smith and I asked her to listen to 'What You Never Know (Won't Hurt You)'.

'What do you think of this?' I asked. 'Do you like it or not?'

'Yeah, I do,' she replied.

'Now, you're not just saying that, are you? I need honesty here.'

'I really like it,' she said. And that was good enough for me.

During the same trip back home, together with the rest of my family, I went camping. Again, I took my collection of CDs to listen to while we were staying in the tent.

Now, camping was a big annual event right through our childhoods. Our family holidays usually began with four or five false starts. As we drove to the end of our driveway, the shout would go up from Mum in the front passenger seat, 'We've forgotten the sunhats!' Around we would turn to pick up the absent items. Then, we would get half an hour away and suddenly Mum would say, 'I don't know if I packed enough summer clothes. It's looking quite sunny now.' Or, 'Sophie's forgotten her sarong. If we don't go back now, we'll have to buy another one.' So, around we would turn again. In the end, it became one of the Westenra family's running jokes. When we finally set off, there was always a horrible seven-hour drive to Golden Bank on the top of New Zealand's South Island.

Dad always drove, with Mum sitting next to him in the front and us three kids squashed into the back. Hitched to the back of the car was our trailer, crammed full with the tent, our bikes and a couple of chilly bins to help keep our food cool.

We tended to go camping in time for New Year's Eve. The plan was to arrive during the day and then to stay up late to see in the New Year. Most families set off around breakfast, so that they could arrive at the campsite in good time, set up their gear and then involve themselves in the festivities. We were never quite as organised as that and would usually arrive under the cover of darkness, which would mean that we would struggle to put up our tent with just the car's headlights and some torches to help us see what we were doing.

Our tent was an ex-demonstration model from a camping store, which we had bought as a Westenra family bargain. When it was finally pitched, the insides quickly took on a home-away-from-home quality, with the amount of para-phernalia that we brought with us growing every year. Mind you, some of the stuff that other campers brought with them, such as portable televisions, always made me wonder why they'd even bothered to go camping in the first place.

We had a little gas stove to cook on, although generally the campsites had kitchens. It became a great social event, as we saw the same families year after year. We had some wonderful times and it was a particularly big adventure when we were small children. Having said that, there were some miserable times, too, when it rained, and we were forced to trudge out through the mud to visit the toilet in the middle of the night, armed only with a torch and an umbrella. I can remember asking myself why we were there when, not so far away, we had a nice, warm, dry house with our own beds. On balance, though, I wouldn't have swapped those camping experiences with Mum, Dad, Sophie and Isaac for anything else in the world.

It sounds very arrogant to me as I write this next sentence, but it's the truth. The main reason why the camping had to stop was that I had become too recognisable for us to be able to stay on the campsite and for me to find the experience in any way a relaxing break. On the first morning after we arrived at the site, I was standing in the queue for a shower in the morning.

'Hey, you're the singer, aren't you?' the woman standing next to me asked excitedly.

I looked embarrassed and mumbled, 'Er, yes, I am,' silently adding, 'And I just want to have my shower. I don't want anyone to recognise me. I've just got out of bed.'

My entire holiday began to centre on avoiding being recognised on the campsite. I think this was the first time that we truly understood the effect of a whole year of television, radio and newspaper reports, relentless advertising and posters in the window of every record store in New Zealand. It's not that I blame people – I realise that they bought my albums and bought into a slice of me in the process. So it was perfectly understandable that they would be intrigued when my family and I pitched our tent on the campsite where they had chosen to spend their holiday.

The trouble was that, once people had located our tent, there was simply no escape. Small groups started to hang out nearby for no good reason at all. Mum had to tell people that I was resting because I was tired, in the hope that they would become bored and go away. We had a family-sized tent with two big rooms and an outside area. Even though we were right on the beach front, which was really beautiful, I spent hours hiding out inside pretending to be asleep so that the visitors would go away. There were hundreds of tents on the campsite, but absolutely everyone seemed to have worked out which one was ours. One young boy even brought around his fish and chips to eat while he waited for me to wake up. He just sat there chatting for ages to my family. It started not to be a holiday for me.

I was at the age where I wanted to hang out with my friends as well. It was by no means a rebellion on my part, but I was keen to exert my teenage independence. This made me kind of resentful that I was on a family holiday where I couldn't even chill out because I was having to be sociable the whole time.

The camping had to stop, and the following year we had a free week's holiday in Australia on the Gold Coast, between two concerts that I had to give, so it worked out really well. We had done the whole camping thing. Now we deserved a bit of luxury, with a bathroom of our own, rather than one we had to share with the whole campsite. Then, in 2006 we rented a house instead, which was great fun and much more civilised.

Being shut away in the back of the tent did give me plenty of listening time and, by the time I returned to London, I was pretty certain about the tracks I wanted to appear on my new album, which once again was produced by Giles Martin. Just as he had done with *Pure*, he made the whole experience very enjoyable and we continued to have a lot of laughs between takes.

We recorded most of the album at Metropolis Studios in London, at the same time as the McFly boys were recording there. As usual, I was excited to be working in the same building as a bunch of chart-topping pop stars. Every morning, I passed a group of girls not much younger than I was, who waited outside the studios, hoping to catch a glimpse of the band. They must have had to hang around for hours just to get the most fleeting of sights of them. I used to feel quite smug about being able to walk into the studio complex and say, 'Hey, guys!' to them. I had met them before, briefly, at a Universal Music sales conference, where we performed in front of the people responsible for selling our records into retailers. It still gave me a buzz to be recording in a studio such as Metropolis – it was such a starry place to be.

I was out on the road soon after *Odyssey* was released, but, rather than my own headline tour, this time I was appearing with Il Divo, the pop-opera quartet created by Simon Cowell, who have been particularly successful in the USA and in countries across Europe. For the American leg of the tour, I had a rock-band setup with drums, guitar, bass and Jeff Franzel on keyboards.

Working alongside Il Divo was a great opportunity for me to meet American audiences in a big way for the first time and also for me to experiment with a more pop-influenced style, rather than the classical-music setup that I had been used to at home in New Zealand and in the UK. We had some rehearsals in a little New York studio before we set off on the road. I loved working with a drummer; it was a novelty for me because most of my arrangements are string-based. It was a different experience and I felt quite pumped up when I heard the strong percussive beat next to me.

While we were in New York, we also spent some time thinking about what I should be wearing on stage. In the end, I opted for black knee-high boots, jeans and a sequinned top. It was a different look from anything I had worn before, and I enjoyed it a lot.

It was quite an adventure being on tour with Sebastian, Carlos, David and Urs – the Il Divo boys. All four of them were unfailingly charming to me – especially Sebastian, who always kept an eye out for me to make sure that I was all right. When I first met them, they all came up to me to introduce themselves individually, which I thought was really sweet. They were very friendly, although I didn't see as much of them on the American leg of the tour as I did when we were in Europe. Initially, I was in my own little world with my band and they were in their zone. We bumped into each other at catering and on the side of the stage when they were running off from their soundcheck and I was going on to do mine.

As I was coming off the stage after performing in Los Angeles, I looked up and saw Simon Cowell walking down a corridor in front of me. He had been meeting with the Il Divo guys. Oh, my goodness! I thought to myself. He's right in front of me. I should introduce myself, I really should. But I bottled it and I was too shy to say a simple 'Hello, I'm Hayley.' I was like a rabbit caught in the headlights. The effect he had on people as he walked past them along the corridor was amazing. He is one of the most instantly recognisable individuals in America and people just stared at him open-mouthed when they saw him. There were lots of people just as starstruck as me, and I would have felt very embarrassed had I gone up to him. That said, given the chance again, I would say hello to him because I admire what he's achieved enormously.

While I was working with Il Divo, I was very lucky to have a tour manager called Ali McMordie, who was a real rock'n'roll kind of guy. I'm sure that I posed far less of a challenge to him than some of the bands he had looked after in the past. His role was to make sure that everything ran smoothly and to see that we were all in the right place at the right time. He also had to sort out any problems that cropped up along the way. Previously, he had been a bass guitarist in a rock group, so he had seen a bit of life. He's the sort of guy who has a very tough exterior, but turns out to be very sweet when you get to know him.

The musicians in the band were all male, so quite often I had to block my ears in the tour bus. It was only when I laughingly shouted out, 'Oh my gosh! I don't need to be hearing this!' that they remembered that they had a lady present. This had its good and bad points, but we had great fun and there was a lot of joking all through the tour.

Working with the band allowed me the opportunity to perform quite differently, and I still incorporate what I learned then into my sets these days. Sometimes, it's good to be thrown into new situations, so that you develop and learn new skills. I really got a handle on talking to audiences on the tour. For a start, I was the support act, so I was warned that, since I was not the main reason that the audience had come to the concert, they might behave differently towards me, for example, by not turning up until halfway through my set. Most of the time, the crowd who turned up to Il Divo's concerts were not your typical rock'n'roll audience and the majority of them were there on time, although there were still people who drifted in late and I had to work hard at grabbing their attention. I enjoyed that challenge because it reminded me of my busking days. I went into the mindset that I had used back in Christchurch, when I knew that I had to stop people in their tracks using nothing but my voice.

I started the show by chatting to the audience a little and I kept things very light throughout. I started off each night with 'She Moves Through the Fair' and then I sang many of my old favourites, although 'Both Sides Now' was the song that really seemed to hit the spot with the audience.

I definitely thrive on applause and the reaction from the audience when I'm on stage. I guess it feeds the ego. As singers go, I don't believe that I have a big ego, though. Because of my upbringing, I'm still quite a humble, down-to-earth sort of person and I know that the rest of my family will always keep me grounded. They would never in a million years let me become big-headed.

I'm not going to name names here, because this is not that sort of book. But, rest assured, as I've travelled around the world, I've come across some really big egos among my fellow recording artists. They behave as if everyone were in second place to them. I can't understand how they fail to see what they're doing and what kind of image they're giving off. Maybe I'm too self-aware for my own good and sometimes I possibly care a little too much about what people think. But, when I hear about some of the antics that some stars get up to, I think, Oh my gosh! How embarrassing to create that much of a scene!

If I rise above myself and look down, I don't see myself as grabbing so frantically at fame as some people, who seem to be desperate to make their mark at any cost. I feel much more sure of my place in this world and the reasons why I'm here. I have some friends in the music industry who can be very sweet people, but they struggle to keep their egos in check. I don't understand how they can be such lovely people one minute and then so unsure of themselves the next. Their behaviour is almost self-destructive.

The really big stars I've worked with – people such as José Carreras and Bryn Terfel – are such warm and friendly people all of the time. Most of the people at the top are fundamentally nice. They've realised that to get to the top and stay there they have to behave in a way that is respectful to those working around them. Nobody does themselves any favours by being nasty. Mind you, I've been told on many occasions, "Sometimes, it's good to be a bit of a diva, because you gain more respect.' I'm not certain that this is true, though, because I'm sure that people just find ways of working *around* a demanding artist, rather than working *with* them. I would hate for that ever to happen to me.

I do have a rider when I'm on tour – this is a list of demands that are part of the contract my management signs with the promoter of each concert that I do. Virtually every singer has some sort of rider and some of them can be extraordinarily excessive and prescriptive, forcing the promoter to jump through all sort of hoops just to keep the artist happy. Rock bands can be particularly demanding, but I reckon most of them do it just to see how far they can push the boundaries of what is acceptable.

My rider is an altogether more simple affair. I always ask for some bottles of room-temperature water. This is common to most singers, because chilled water affects the vocal cords. Then, I ask for a selection of fresh fruit, crudities, dips and crackers. Finally, I request a can of wild salmon and an avocado. I also stipulate that I need a can opener in the contract, because you have no idea how many times I've been unable to get at the salmon that has been provided for me, because nobody left a can opener behind. I never ask for alcohol because I never drink alcohol when I'm performing. My one luxury is that I ask for all the fruit and vegetables to be organic if possible. I also like things to be left in the packets, so that I know that they really are fresh and organic. And that's it! I'm sure that the backstage people in some concert halls think I'm odd because I ask for so little.

I have to admit that I'm a bit strange when it comes to my eating habits. I try to make a real effort to stay healthy because I'm always travelling. One of my vices however is Green & Black's organic dark chocolate. Somehow, my biggest fans have found this out and I usually end up with a few bars of chocolate after every concert. I tend to share it with the rest of the team in the van on the way back home.

After the final night of the American tour, Il Divo headed off to Australia and, unfortunately, I was unable to go with them, because I was committed to performing a few concerts of my own in America. In some ways, it was a little disappointing, because Australia is almost (but not quite) home territory for me and it would have been great to have appeared there with the boys, because my Aussie friends always give me such a great reception whenever I perform there.

After my concerts in America, I needed to head straight back to rejoin Il Divo for the European leg of the tour. We were heading for Dublin, but our first flight from Florida had been delayed for about three hours, so we missed our connecting flight. It meant that my tour manager Ali and I ended up somewhere in the middle of America, trying to find a way to Dublin in time for the concert. Even if our travel plans had gone like clockwork, we were already cutting it fine, but the added delays meant that there was a real risk of my not making the concert at all. That would have meant letting too many people down, so we had to get there at all costs.

As we looked up at the indicator boards at the airport, we realised that more and more flights were being cancelled because of bad weather. There were no direct flights to Dublin and we were given two options: either we could fly to Paris and pick up a connecting flight there, or else we could fly to London Heathrow and then pick up a plane to Dublin from London Gatwick. We chose the latter option and my management had a fast car waiting for us at the airport, which zoomed us across London.

I sank into my seat on the final flight, safe in the knowledge that, so long as the plane touched down on time, I would just be able to make the arena in time for my performance. A man sitting near to me leaned across and politely asked, 'Excuse me, but you're not Hayley Westenra, are you?'

'Yes, I am,' I answered.

'You're doing a show tonight with Il Divo?'

'Yep!' I said with a look of exasperation in my eyes. It turned out that my fellow passenger was also going along to the concert – although he was planning to watch it, rather than perform in it – and so he was arriving at the right time. I gave him a little shout out from the stage as I told the story of my travel nightmares to the audience later that night.

We landed at the right time, in the right place and I was convinced that nothing else could possibly go wrong, since we had about three hours to spare before the show. Then, as I waited at the luggage carousel, I discovered that my bags had not made it to Dublin with me and were still somewhere back in London. I have Mum to thank for the fact that this was not the major catastrophe that at first it appeared to be. She constantly reminds me to take a dress and a pair of shoes with me in my hand luggage whenever I'm travelling to a show. Fortunately, on this occasion, I had heeded her advice. It meant that I had something to wear when I went on stage.

I stopped off at the airport branch of Accessorize and bought myself some shiny jewellery that would sparkle under the lights while I was performing. When I arrived at the Point arena, Carol Wright, a lovely lady from my record label who had flown over to Dublin from London to oversee my European Il Divo tour debut, kindly rushed out to buy me some hairspray and I borrowed other bits and pieces from a variety of different people to enable me to go on stage still looking the part.

I had time for only the briefest of soundchecks, which was a bit of a challenge, since on this leg of the tour I was singing different material to a backing track, rather than with a live band. It was a case of really being thrown in at the deep end – not only had I arrived late, but I was going on stage to a whole new setup.

In the end, it all went smoothly and the audience would have been none the wiser had I not regaled them with tales of my intercontinental flight nightmare.

Over the next few weeks, as we travelled around Europe, I got to know the Il Divo guys a little better. I no longer had my band with me, so I ended up mixing with their crew a little more. It was another all-male environment, other than me, the wardrobe lady, the hair and makeup lady and the monitor engineer. I quickly formed a bond with the sound guys that they used, who were nearly all Aussies. Usually, there's a healthy rivalry between Australians and New Zealanders, but, when we are in the northern hemisphere, we Antipodeans like to stick together.

I found that one of the attractive elements of being on a long tour is that I was able to focus on the concerts every night, which allowed me to develop a real sense of momentum. On other occasions, I've a more sporadic set of concerts over a couple of months, which I juggle with other work such as press interviews, promotional appearances and recording. Both of these styles of concert-giving have their pluses and minuses. The big danger with a full-on tour is that you can be dragged down by just how far you have got to travel and the sheer number of concerts that you have ahead of you. I would hate to be counting down concerts to the end of a tour. You don't want to be in that mindset because it means that you are not enjoying every moment.

On the positive side, with a big tour, you are performing virtually every night and you soon get into a routine. I found that this meant that I could experiment a little with the music, instead of worrying about other aspects of my performance, such as what I was going to say between tracks, for example. When I was younger, I used to mumble on stage, but now I enjoy developing my banter with the audience. I'm always on the lookout for a good joke. I have to admit that, when I come across a joke that is well received, I try to get my money's worth from it. It does make me worry for the handful of very loyal fans who come to more than one performance, but I always hope that they understand that a good joke is hard to find!

One of the other highlights for me on *Odyssey* was 'Dell'amore Non Si Sa', the duet I recorded with Andrea Bocelli. I felt very privileged when he agreed to come on my album. In fact it was more than that: it was a huge personal thrill for me. I had been singing along to his albums for years. And then, suddenly to have his name on my album was like 'Wow!'

Just after I finished touring with Il Divo, I was given the opportunity to perform with Andrea at some of his concerts. He has one of the most remarkable voices that I've ever heard and is a completely charming man. He was always very generous to me on stage. Singing with him was one of the most significant events of another busy year for me.

CHAPTER 10
BICYCLES FOR GHANA

It was just after my first international album, *Pure*, had become a success that I was approached by Dennis McKinley, who headed UNICEF New Zealand, and asked whether I would be interested in becoming a Goodwill Ambassador for them. Usually this honour goes to people far, far older than I am, and I discovered that if I accepted I would be one of the youngest people to have taken up the role.

Initially, I was a little reluctant to accept because I felt that it was a huge responsibility. I've always been adamant that I'll not simply become a 'face' that is associated with a large number of different charities, causes and campaigns, without actually doing anything of any significance to support them. If I was to take on a role like that, I really wanted to do my bit. I wondered whether I would have time to fit it into my hectic schedule of international travel. In the end, I came to the conclusion that it was such a fantastic organisation, performing such valuable work around the globe, that I would do everything I could to help them.

UNICEF work primarily in the developing world, although they do have projects and programmes that are aimed at New Zealanders. I was particularly attracted to their work because of its focus on children and its relevance to people of my age. I hope that it might be good for the charity to have a young person flying the UNICEF flag. It's probably easier for someone in their late teens or early twenties to relate to the young people that UNICEF helps than it is for someone in their forties or fifties.

Initially, I found it quite hard to promote their work because I didn't have first-hand experience of what they achieve. I was desperate to go on a field trip because I didn't feel that I could talk knowledgeably about the positive effects that a UNICEF programme can have on a community, having only watched the documentaries and read the brochures that everyone else had read. I wanted to feel that I had the authority to talk about UNICEF's work, so I was very excited when the opportunity arose for me to visit Ghana. As it turned out, I would end up playing a far more practical role in helping a group of people than I had ever expected.

In total, I spent five days in Ghana: three days in Accra and two days in Tamale. Mum, Sophie, my manager Steve and I all flew out on a regular flight from London. The first thing that struck me when we got off the plane was that, even though we were in a city, it seemed quieter and more rural. It was also far, far hotter than it had been in London, even though we arrived in the dark, so we were unable to see much. Everything felt slightly more primitive than the world that we had left behind and the pace of life seemed slower. We were waved through passport control by the two guys sitting behind the desk – there certainly was no sign of the queues that I've become used to at London Heathrow.

We were met by the son of the chairman of UNICEF in Ghana and some other members of the UNICEF team. We were driven to our hotel, which seemed to be a fairly standard, comfortable sort of place. It was frequented by the air crews while they were resting between flights and by foreign businesspeople in town for meetings. It didn't feel that different from many of the other hotels I've stayed in, although perhaps the rooms were a little more basic than we would have at home. At breakfast the next morning, the selection of food on offer was not quite as extensive as we might normally be used to.

There was nothing about the look and feel of the hotel that would prepare us for what we would see later that day. We began the morning with a briefing from the UNICEF team, who filled us in on the situation in Ghana. The battle to eradicate polio was one of the major aims of the charity's presence in the country. Education was also a big issue there, with a particular imbalance when it came to the number of girls and boys who were attending school. It's a problem that is widespread in developing countries, because families don't see the need to educate their daughters, and this leads to a real inequality. As soon as I heard about the problem, I wondered whether there was something that I could do to help.

We were driven from the hotel out through the city streets. It was by now even hotter than it had been the night before. The city was dusty and very dry; everywhere around us were people walking the streets carrying baskets filled with mangoes and plantain. I felt like a real foreigner because I'm very pale and not suited to that sort of climate at all. Our white Land Rover had 'UNICEF' painted in large letters along the side and, as we drove through the streets, we would always be greeted with warm smiles. The local children ran alongside as we drove, calling up and waving to us. It was easy to see the affection and respect that UNICEF generates on the ground because of its long history of successful programmes in Ghana.

It made me start to think about the whole concept of being a 'celebrity' – and, in particular, the culture that surrounds celebrity in developed countries. Certainly, the kids whom I met in Ghana had no idea about fame; instead, they understood that UNICEF were a group of people who could unlock the door to their growing up with the prospect of a better future.

The single most exciting thing for the children we met seemed to be the opportunity to have their photograph taken and then seeing themselves on the screen of the digital camera. As soon as they caught sight of themselves it gave them a real thrill. Steve still cherishes some video footage of a group of Ghanaian children jumping up and down and chanting 'Luton! Luton! Luton!' – the name of his beloved football team back home in England.

Sophie brought over a selection of presents for the local children, including skipping ropes and pens, both of which caused a burst of huge excitement, and a soccer ball, which propelled the excitement level to a point of frenzy. It was amazing to see how such simple gifts were greeted with such enormous gratitude. We also handed out sunglasses, caps and toy cars. The kids got such a thrill out of each of these items, all of which were far less extravagant than the presents given to children in developed countries.

We were accompanied on our trip by a journalist from the New Zealand *Women's Weekly* magazine and a film crew from a New Zealand programme called *Close Up*. They were documenting our travels. One of the first places we visited was the city slums. This was an eye-opening experience. People are living in appallingly grim conditions, forced to make homes for themselves out of corrugated-iron sheets, or any other materials that they can lay their hands on. There's no sanitation at all, so the stench was overpowering. The people living there look unhealthy and dirty. Some are dressed in torn rags; others wear clothes that have been sent over from the Western world. The logos and slogans emblazoned on their T-shirts seem completely at odds with the environment in which they find themselves.

However, it's amazing how adaptable human beings can be. We met one lady who had her own home, which was nothing more than a shed. My instinctive first reaction was to pity her, but she greeted us with a smile. She was proud to show us her home. There were two television sets inside and this confused me. But it turned out that they didn't actually work and had been scavenged from other people's rubbish. For that particular woman, they were here possessions, her belongings, and, because of that, she was very proud of them

I had a tremendous sense of guilt throughout the trip. As I was shown around, I felt that I wanted to make immediate changes.

Wouldn't it be amazing to give this lady her own clean house that's not part of a slum? I thought to myself.

I regretted not bringing with me something that could have made a difference, even if it were only some money to help provide her with the opportunity to take a step up the ladder. But the problem comes as you spend more time in the country. Gradually, I met more and more people like her and the scale of the problem suddenly dawned on me. It became quite overwhelming and I found it a very emotional experience. I'm not ashamed to say that I shed a tear before

I went to sleep that night, as much out of frustration at the size of the job that had to be done as a response to the individual sights I had seen and stories I had heard.

As well as polio, the children there develop distension of the stomach, which is brought about by a lack of protein, I believe. Even so, the younger children still smile and chatter away. I found it truly amazing that they were brimming with energy and always appeared excited about life, despite their surroundings. Back in the developed would, many children simply don't realise how lucky they are. They can be grumpy and walk around with sour looks on their faces, but the young Ghanaian children were excited to be at school; they revelled in learning.

As the Ghanaians became older, though, I think they gained a greater perspective on the tough realities that life would throw at them. I met many girls aged between fourteen and seventeen and it was easy to see that by this age they had already been hardened to the world by what they had seen and experienced. They seemed to have lost hope.

The contrast between the younger children and the older teenagers was brought home to me on one particular day. First, we went to a school where we met a group of bright-eyed five-year-olds. They all carried their own chalk-boards for writing on and they loved drawing in chalk on one another's face. They had a huge sense of optimism and they were keen and very affectionate. The whole classroom was filled with good-natured organised chaos.

Then I met a group of girls who had been taken off the streets by UNICEF. All of the naïve enthusiasm exhibited by the five-year-olds had by now completely evaporated. UNICEF specifically set up a school to encourage the girls to become engaged with the education system. Many of these girls came into the big city from the rural areas in the hope of earning more money for their families. There's a steady stream of them, who believe that they will be able to discover work in the city, but instead they find themselves open to attack and abuse.

They have no roof above their heads and nobody looking out for them. HIV and AIDS have often ravaged their families, with both parents dying in many cases. This is a common problem that keeps the girls at home, unable to go to school, because they end up being forced to take on the parenting role for very young children who have nobody else to care for them.

UNICEF have discovered that, as the attendance rates of girls in schools was raised, so the infant mortality rate was lowered. This correlation comes about because the girls are taught both how to protect themselves from HIV and also a whole range of life skills that would normally be passed on by their parents, including how to look after children. I was initially shocked to learn that girls as young as nine were taught about the dangers of HIV and AIDS and were also given training in how to pass on their knowledge to other students their age. However, it's an absolute necessity because this terrible disease is such an issue there.

During my visit, I learned about a UNICEF project to provide girls with bicycles to help them to get to school. Many of them have long journeys each way every day – and this can be another barrier to their attending classes. They are open to attack when they are on foot and it's much safer and easier for them if they are on a bike. They are also able to use the bicycles to help them complete other household chores, such as fetching water from the local borehole.

It's exclusively girls who are given the bikes, and I instantly became very taken with this project. While I was there, I told the UNICEF team that I would like to adopt Bicycles for Ghana as the focus for my charity work. I felt that it was an idea that people back home would grasp on to because it was raising money for something tangible.

Rather than just donating to a cause and seeing money disappear into an organisation, fundraisers would be able to see exactly where their money was going, bicycle by bicycle.

I felt that people would particularly relate to the project in New Zealand, where virtually every kid owns a bike. Even if the kids back home didn't quite understand how and why the bicycles would help, I was sure that they would connect with the idea that the Ghanaian girls would gain a lot of pleasure from the bikes.

My feelings were proved right. Since then, I've given concerts where the profits have gone to UNICEF. On my latest New Zealand tour, two dollars from every ticket were donated to the project. The support from my fans has been amazing, with schools and cycling clubs around the world helping to raise funds. It really seems to have captured people's imaginations. At the time of writing this book, six thousand bicycles have already been distributed, and UNICEF are in the process of buying many thousands more.

It was after our visit to the city slum that I actually saw the bicycles in action. We travelled to Tamale, which was far more rural than what we had seen before. We were introduced to a village community, where the people's main drinking source was a pond. The water was coffee-coloured. I watched as children scooped it out with plastic containers or possibly coconut shells. They lifted it straight to their lips and drank it.

As this was going on, it was explained to me that the water was infested with Guinea worm larvae. If these are ingested, the worms grow inside the human body. I was shocked to see children with open wounds, from which the Guinea worm is trying to escape. To try to work the worm out of the body, they wrap it around a stick and twist it a little each day. It was horrific. I met one girl who couldn't go to school because the wounds on her feet caused by the Guinea worm were so painful that she was unable to walk.

To help counter the problem, UNICEF provide nets for straining the water in the pond. They then educate people on how and why they need to use them, but, even then, this is by no means a 100 per cent effective method for getting rid of the larvae. Really, they just need clean drinking water – and this means more boreholes and pumps to allow them to access it.

As I watched the children playing around the pond, I looked down at my bag and the bottle of clean, crystal clear mineral water that I never go anywhere without. I felt so guilty that something we take for granted that comes pouring out of our taps at home every day, on demand, is such a precious commodity for these people.

The local people were just as welcoming as they had been in the city. Here, they put on a song-and-dance performance for me. They were infectiously enthusiastic and I joined in the dancing, although I didn't have a clue what I was doing. The dance mainly consisted of bumping hips with the woman standing next to you and they loved the fact that I joined in. When it was time to leave, they gave us such a fantastic send-off, with the whole community out singing us goodbye.

We travelled on and I sang at our next stop for a little girl aged around twelve and her father, who was blind. He was so appreciative and moved. I then gave an impromptu performance for the chief of the area where we were. In return, he offered me my own piece of land and two chickens. I didn't know quite how to react to that, but I felt quite honoured. It was very humbling because they have so little, but even what they do have they offer to give away. Sophie gave a girl of around her age a pen and the girl gave her a little bracelet in return. Through UNICEF, they have kept in touch ever since and have become pen pals.

The highlight of the trip for me was when we went to a school, where we met a group of girls who had been given bicycles by UNICEF. In fact, there was a whole fleet of them. Mum had been keenly documenting the trip with her camera and she decided that it would be useful to have a photograph of me with the girls and a bike, so that we could use it to publicise the appeal back home. It was decided that it would be a good idea if I was photographed holding on to a bicycle, so we asked if we could borrow one from one of the girls. She was extremely reluctant to let it go and our translator had to explain why we needed it and to reassure her that she would get it back. At that moment, I realised just how important these bicycles were to the girls.

Next, we decided to stage a bicycle race for the television crew. The idea was that I wouldn't do the whole race, but they thought that it would be a great opportunity to shoot some footage of me with the other girls and their bicycles. I was instructed to join in at the end of the race, so that I could appear in the centre of the shots. We were a bit worried that I would be left far behind if I tried to take part in the whole race. It turned out that the last part of the race included a patch of dirt track that turned around a corner on to a gravel path.

I waited patiently on the dirt track, feeling a little ashamed that I was not competing in the whole race and utterly convinced that the other girls were probably thinking, Hey! She's cheating! I hoped that the translator had explained properly that they just wanted some film and some photographs. As the girls came hurtling towards me, I began pedalling. I was not used to the bicycles and I was not used to the terrain either. Had I not been clinging on for dear life, I would have been crossing my fingers in the hope that the crew got the shots they needed and I wouldn't have to do it again.

We made a right turn from the dirt track on to the gravel path at quite some speed. I skidded and went flying off the bike. I landed in a heap on the ground with a huge red graze on my leg and a large red stain from the earth all down the front of my UNICEF T-shirt. It was all on camera and one day I fully expect to see the footage on one of those television outtake programmes. Remembering my song-and-dance training from Canterbury Youth Opera days, I picked myself up and climbed back on the bike with a fixed grin on my face, even though I was crying inside. It was not until the crew had the shots that they needed that I dismounted and admitted just how painful my leg felt. My pride was also a little dented because it was quite apparent that they were all much better cyclists than I was.

After I had dusted myself down, I was asked to present prizes to the students who had been performing well at school. In another humbling moment, it was touching to see how delighted the girls were to be given fresh exercise books as prizes. They then presented me with a turban-like headdress and a dress that wrapped around the body. They were thrilled when I asked them to help me to put them on. We gave them some skipping ropes and a big bag of lollipops, which they loved.

The time I spend with UNICEF feels very worthwhile, but I always have this sense that there's more to be done. I feel incredibly passionate about the work that they do. There are some amazing people who work in countries like Ghana for UNICEF. When you meet them, you immediately realise that this is so much more than just a job for them and they are doing a lot more than they are paid to do.

I came away from Ghana wanting to do all that I could to help them. When I saw how people live there, it was not a surprise, but it was still a shock. I found it very hard to prepare myself for some of the scenes. I knew it would be tough, but in the end I was there for only five days. It sounds terrible to admit, but by the end of the trip I was relieved to be going home because I found it so draining. On the flight home, I felt guilty for feeling that way. I should have wanted to stay there longer.

It was by no means all doom and gloom. I really gained a sense of how UNICEF make a difference. I met girls whose lives had been changed. They had gained an education; they had been given free meals; they had learned the skills to help them to set up their own businesses; and then they had travelled back to their villages able to share what they had learned with other girls facing similar hardships to themselves.

I wish everyone living in a developed country could go to see life in a developing one. I wish they could meet the people in places like Ghana and have their eyes opened. I've done it and now it's something that I can tell people about first-hand. That is why the trip meant so much to me.

I left Ghana far more motivated to make a difference. I hope that we will achieve real change in girls' lives there through the bicycle project and I'm looking forward to going back to Ghana soon to see how the money that we raise is being spent.

CHAPTER 11
TREASURE

Each time I sit down and start to think about recording a new album, I always want to ensure that it's better than everything that has gone before, both in the sense of the repertoire that I choose to include and in terms of my own vocal performance. As I mentioned earlier, I had intended to write more of my second Decca album, *Odyssey*, myself. But it was not to be. I was determined that I really would make my mark as a songwriter on my new album, *Treasure*.

By this stage I had done a lot of touring and I had developed an acute understanding of which songs worked the best for my audiences. It's funny, but the songs that I perform the best are often the ones that I'm most comfortable with. In turn, these seem to be the songs that resonate most strongly with the audiences. A good example of this is 'Prayer', which is one of the main tracks I perform from *Odyssey*. It always creates a beautiful atmosphere at a concert and I can tell that the audience are enjoying listening to it as much as I delight in singing it. It's one of those songs that connect audience and singer; together we can revel in the music.

Initially, for *Treasure*, I wanted to create more of this type of song and home in on the sound that works best with my audiences. So, I started to write more tracks of my own that could possibly be included on the album. Then, some way down this process, I hit upon a slightly different central core to my new disc.

My inspiration was Nanna. She means an awful lot to me and was an incredibly significant part of my musical life while I was growing up. So, I made a list of songs that she used to perform in her singing days. *Treasure* then became an album with a dual role. As well as a set of new songs to keep my repertoire moving forward, I would also record some of the hits that were big in Nanna's repertoire and that I felt deserved to be kept alive in the public's conscience.

It's great to be recording songs that have been around for years, but I felt that I had reached a point as an artist when I wanted to be representing the music of the present time. So the tracks on *Treasure* showcase how I feel now. I also wanted to sing some songs that nobody else could claim to have sung first. They are mine and mine alone, and, if other people record them later down the track, then that will be fantastic, but they will always be 'Hayley's songs'.

With a song such as 'Danny Boy', which has been sung many times by many different people, I wanted to try to come at the words and the music from a fresh place. Whenever I perform it live, I try to draw the audience into the story. The music is still relatively new to me because of my age, and, in the new arrangements I used on the album, I've attempted to put a fresh spin on it.

The same can be said for 'One Fine Day', which comes from Giacomo Puccini's opera *Madame Butterfly*. I'm always very conscious of the fact that, while I'm young, my voice is still not fully developed. This means that there are some operatic arias that I should not tackle yet. 'One Fine Day', which is another of Nanna's favourites, is a challenge for me in some respects, but it's certainly within my range. I don't want to be in the situation where I play it too safe, so that I fail to set new vocal challenges for myself along the way.

I wrote the first track on *Treasure*, called 'Let Me Lie', while I was staying at Daniel Bedingfield's house in London. He and the rest of his family have become great friends of mine over the past few years, but I would like to take this opportunity to lay to rest once and for all the rumours that we enjoyed a romantic relationship. We met at the Royal Variety Performance in Edinburgh. I was in awe of his performance. He's such a fantastic singer and songwriter. I didn't realise that he was born in New Zealand, but after the show we got talking and he told me that he was also a Kiwi by birth.

Shortly after we met, he had a terrible car accident in New Zealand and was quite badly hurt. I sent him flowers on behalf of the Westenra family, wishing him well. Suddenly, there was an article in one of the British tabloid newspapers, saying that I was hanging around by his hospital bedside and that we were going out, but had yet to kiss because of his head brace. Very quickly, the news also made the papers in New Zealand. Friends started to come up to me at school saying, 'Why didn't you tell us?' Daniel had friends texting him saying, 'You didn't tell us about Hayley.' But there was absolutely no truth in the story, and it was a PR stunt by somebody.

If you were hoping to read pages of lurid details about my love life in this book, then by now you have probably worked out that you're going to be disappointed. It has never been easy dating people. It started when I was at school, when I was always the short-arse. Because I was a little squirt, the guys were never really that interested in me, anyway. Mum was always short as a child too, so she could relate to it. She would often say, 'Hayley, one day your prince will come' – but that didn't make it any less frustrating at the time.

Putting that stumbling block to one side, I've basically been on the road ever since I started making albums. I've had the opportunity to meet lots of amazing people and I can absolutely assure you that I've been out on my fair share of dates. I usually spend very little time in one place and my work tends to take up all of my spare time.

It's hard enough for any girl to find Mr Right, but I'm definitely not the sort of person who goes out with guys just for the sake of going out with them. I'm not going to hang out with someone just to pass the time of day either, so, if I go out with someone and it's not working, I'll call it a day because there's no point in carrying on under false pretences. I've never really had a serious relationship, but I do think that if I arrive at the point when I think that my work has completely taken over, and that I'll never find anyone, then I'll sort myself out. And I don't intend to wait until I'm 72 years old for that to happen!

It used to make me feel a bit disheartened that I didn't have a guy, but I do believe that I've rationalised it now. I've no idea whom I'll end up with and I've no ideal man in my head. I have a feeling that I'm going to come across someone through a completely chance encounter, maybe randomly on a train or in the supermarket. It takes years for some people to find their soulmate. I have friends in their thirties who are still looking for someone. So, at the age of just twenty, I'm not too worried yet. Time is still on my side. It's not as if I were living the life of a hermit, either. I'm going out, meeting people and having a good time. As a good friend said to me, 'You have to kiss a lot of toads before you find your prince!'

When you're in the public eye, it does occur to you that someone might be interested only because of the attractions of fame, and I suppose that might be why I tend to be drawn to singers. I used to be completely convinced that I would end up with a musician, but I now wonder whether a relationship made up from two performers might be doomed from the outset unless they really are comfortable with the fact that one or other of them might be more or less successful at different times in their lives.

So, just to reiterate: Daniel Bedingfield, with whom I had a completely platonic friendship, came to one of my concerts in Auckland and took me under his wing when I came to the UK. I spent some time staying at his home in London. It was great because they had a piano and it was a very inspirational environment for writing songs. His sister Nikola was there writing her own material and there was always music being played, with a stream of Daniel's musician friends dropping by.

I was sitting inside writing some lyrics when I looked out of the window and saw how beautiful a day it was outside. The sun was shining brightly and the skies were blue. I walked into the garden and lay down on the grass. I felt completely at peace with the world. Suddenly this lyric popped into my head, so I raced back inside and scribbled it down:

Let me lie on grasses green;
On my mother earth I lean.

My rest in the sunshine was over and I worked on the lyric some more, before jumping on to the piano stool and picking out a tune. The melody came very easily and then the rest of the lyric flowed. I wrote the words to the first verse, then the melody and then the words to the chorus, in that order. It was a fantastic moment of creativity and I was very proud of what I had written. Some people may say it's a bit of a 'hippie chick' song, but that doesn't bother me at all and I'm proud to admit that I'm very interested in green issues and conservation. In fact, I'm now a 'matron' for WEN – the Women's Environmental Network.

I took the lyric and melody to 'Let Me Lie' to Sarah Class, who had worked on many of the arrangements on *Pure*. She's also a hippie chick, which is one of the reasons I bonded so well with her. We clicked because she's also a big fan of organic food, alternative therapies and healthy eating in general. Sarah helped me to take 'Let Me Lie' to the next level. We worked on it together, changing the pace of the song and the arrangement of the music. I found her guidance invaluable because, when you are just starting out, it takes a lot to complete a song and sometimes it's useful to have the input of somebody else.

It remains very much my song with the lyric and melody all my own. Once I started writing, I needed to have a publishing company, so, if you look at *Treasure* closely, you'll notice that many of the songs are published by Aroha Music, *aroha* being one of my favourite words – it means 'love' in Maori.

Another of the songs that I co-wrote on *Treasure* has a slightly more accidental origin to its name. 'Le Notte del Silenzio' is Italian for 'The Night of Silence'. However, the song was always intended to be called 'Le Note del Silenzio', which translates as 'The Note of Silence'. But somewhere along the way there was a spelling mistake and the new name stuck.

Once it had appeared everywhere, we decided not to change it, to save even more confusion all round. I wrote it in London with a guy called Antonio Galbiati. We sat around a piano and worked together on it in a very organic way. I loved the creative process, which was a real fusion of Italy and New Zealand. Each time we worked out how a section of the song would sound, we recorded it into a Dictaphone. It remains one of my favourite tracks on the album, even though the name went wrong.

It just goes to show how disorganised this industry is. It's totally dependent on people not making mistakes. Before I made my first record, I had always assumed that every CD that was produced was highly crafted and well thought out; now I think that some of the ones that do well succeed more through fluke than anything else. Quite often it's down to the efforts or decisions of one individual in the team. Albums that bomb can come down to one person making a few stupid mistakes.

Just one wrong decision over release dates; the amount of money available to spend on marketing; the priorities within a record company; even whether the person who originally signed an artist has left the record company in the meantime – all of these can be reasons why otherwise strong albums fail completely. I've seen this happen to other artists so often that I do like to have a say in every part of the record-making process. On the odd occasion when I've handed over an element of control, I've always come to regret it later.

I co-wrote the track 'Summer Rain' with Jeff Franzel, who had worked on the Il Divo tour. As we travelled around America, we would snatch opportunities to write together on our days off. Jeff would often ask, 'Shall we write tomorrow?' and I would agree, while thinking to myself, Bother, there go my shopping plans! or, I just want to sleep and rest my voice. It was a real battle to find time to do some writing and Jeff instilled some strong discipline into me. Otherwise, I might well have kept on procrastinating.

The day that we wrote 'Summer Rain' was an especially good one, because not only did I write a song but I also had time to squeeze in some shopping for a pair of black boots, which was a bonus! I'm not usually that much of a shopper, but, while I was touring with Il Divo, I did enjoy getting out and about in each new city that we visited. I wrote the lyric for the song and then worked on the music with Jeff. Once we were happy with everything, Jeff took the track back home to New York and put it down as a demo, with computer-based instrumentation, so that we could play it to everyone. I particularly liked the pizzicato strings that we eventually worked into the introduction and the way that the strings acted in a percussive way all the way through.

For 'Summer Rain', I wrote the entire lyric on my own and then Jeff and I worked jointly on the music. Creating a song with a co-writer like this is by far my preferred way of operating. I've found that, when I work with a co-writer on the words, it's a less satisfying process. There's no right or wrong way of writing lyrics and it's true to say that another writer can often come up with a great line, but I found that there was always a danger that the song wouldn't end up being what I had initially envisaged it as being. One new line can take the whole story of a song in a different direction.

I suppose it's my controlling nature kicking in, but I find that at this point my interest in the song begins to lessen, I suppose because it's then less personal to me. This was not the case with 'Summer Rain' – it was a great partnership with Jeff that flowed really well, just as it had been when I worked with Antonio on 'Le Notte del Silenzio'.

'Melancholy Interlude' is one of the more unusual tracks on the album. For a start, it lasts for just over a minute and a half. Secondly, it's based on a tune written by the English composer John Dowland, who was born almost five hundred years ago. I came across his piece 'Melancholy Galliard' on an album that I was listening to on my laptop late one night after a concert in Japan. It arrested my attention as soon as I heard it. The melody was very simple but very haunting, and its potential as the basis for a song just grabbed me instantly and I started to sketch out some words.

Steve was just a few doors down from me in the hotel and I knew that he wouldn't be asleep because he always works on his emails until long into the night. I called him up in a state of high excitement.

'Steve, guess what. I've just found a brilliant tune for the album and have some words to match!' I screeched at him down the phone.

'OK, come down and play it to me,' he said.

So I got dressed and walked down the corridor to his room. Once I had sung him through it, he said, 'Well, you'd better record it, so that it doesn't disappear from your mind.'

We recorded a very rough demo on to his computer of this new version of the main theme to 'Melancholy Galliard'. It made it on to the album in a slightly shortened version from the original one that I recorded, but everyone agreed that it worked better like this – very much as an interlude between the main songs.

Once I had selected all of the songs for *Treasure*, it was time to go into the studio again to record the album. This time, I worked with a great new producer, Nick Patrick, who also created a lot of the orchestral arrangements for the album. Nick is one of the most experienced producers of the contemporary classical sound. The orchestra was recorded out in Dublin and I laid down some of the vocal tracks there, with the rest of them being recorded at the studio in Nick's home near Salisbury. Initially, I was not too keen on travelling two hours out of London to make the album, but it helped me to have a really clear headspace and the scenery and countryside around Salisbury was lovely. We made the final part of the album in London, where I worked alongside a choir on one of the tracks.

Since *Treasure* was released towards the beginning of 2007, I've continued to write songs. I'm trying to build up a collection of tracks that I could record myself or that could be recorded by another artist in the future, but singing remains at the centre of everything I do. There was no better reminder of this for me than when *Treasure* had its American launch at an Irish bar called Ulysses in New York. When I look back on that I night, I would count it as being among my favourite performances of all time.

It was not a star-studded occasion, but instead I was able to sing alongside some fantastic musicians playing keyboards, guitar and violin. I had so much fun working with them. The owner of the bar was called Danny and it was his birthday on the night that I was there, so his whole family were there, including his wife and his little daughter, who was sitting on his lap. One of my final tracks was 'Danny Boy', which I dedicated to him. It was a very intimate venue and, as I sang, I could clearly see how much the song meant to him and his family. That simple emotional response to a song that I was singing made it a very special evening for me. The atmosphere was amazing and I could see that night how much my singing could touch people. I felt very honoured to have had that experience.

When it came to launching *Treasure* in the UK, it was accompanied by a press story that really seemed to capture the media's attention. It came about when I was at Steve's house practising my singing. I was worried that if I did it at my place I would disturb the neighbours.

Steve has a lovely dog, brilliantly named Iggy Pup, who is trained not to bark. However, whenever I sing, he starts yelping. Initially, I took offence at this, remembering the effect that my singing had on Zac, my pet cockatiel, back home in Christchurch, who always used to go into a frenzy of squawking whenever I sang. Steve was very interested in the phenomenon and researched it. He discovered that I may have what is known as 'whistle tone'. This is nothing to do with singing beyond the range of human hearing. Instead, it's about having a certain timbre to your voice that animals pick up on. This is far more prevalent with the higher register of a girl's voice. It created quite a stir when the story appeared in *The Times*, and I'm still asked about it when I give interviews now.

With the release of each of my albums, I sense that my fan base widens slightly. If I said that it was only one or two groups of people who buy my records and come to my concerts, then I would be missing out huge tranches of my audience. As well as my official website, www.hayley westenra.com, which is operated by Decca, some of my most loyal fans have got together to create an unofficial fansite at www.hayley-westenra-international.com. The team behind it are very dedicated and they often know more about my schedule than I do. Unfortunately, Keith Sheel and Simon Smalley, two of the leading lights of the site, have both passed away recently. When I get time, I scan the forums to gauge reaction to a particular song or performance. I know that this sounds crazy, but occasionally, if I have a concert coming up that I want to know more about, I log on to the site because I know that the webmasters will have done their research. So, if there's any doubt or confusion over a concert, I always check out what the site has to say.

Most of the moderators on the fansite are UK-based and I always find a big group of HWI people waiting for me at the stage door after my British concert dates. They used to wear a blue sweatshirt with a yellow embroidered HAYLEY

WESTENRA INTERNATIONAL logo on it. Things have moved a little more upmarket now, though, after one of my Scottish fans designed a Westenra tartan especially for me, which was very flattering. So, now the site members all arrive at my concerts sporting a subtle blue and red tartan tie. I keep thinking that one day, perhaps for when I'm performing in Scotland, I should have a kilt made in the Westenra tartan for me to wear on stage.

Most of my fans are absolutely lovely. They tend to be very polite and respectful and I do appreciate it when people come up to me to say hello or to tell me that they have enjoyed one of my albums or concerts. But I'm afraid that I've also experienced a more unsavoury side to being in the public eye, which caused me a good few sleepless nights.

I'm always happy to meet and chat to fans at the signings that are organised around tours or CD releases, but there were a couple of fans in Germany who caused my management and family a lot of concern and kept me on edge for quite some time. Although the two fans both happen to come from Germany, they are completely unrelated to each other.

One started to send me weird fan mail with strange gifts and some sick letters. My management asked the relevant security people to keep an eye on him. He then began to turn up to signings and act weirdly, so security around me at these sorts of events had to be increased.

To be honest, it feels very scary when someone gets that fanatical and when you know that mentally they are not right. You begin to ask yourself what they are capable of. Although I'm usually very level-headed and not prone to panic, I did find the thought of this terrifying.

To an extent, I've been sheltered from some of the details of these kinds of incidents by my management, whom I trust implicitly to sort them out for me. I do know that there are periods when the security around me has to be tightened considerably to deal with the issue. I find that saddening more than anything else, because I know that the vast majority of my fans are wonderful people.

The main incidents have involved another fan from Germany who came to the security people's attention when he began harassing audience members outside one of my concerts in London. He had travelled all the way from Germany and, in the end, he was arrested and the police took him away and put him on a train home. Somehow, he managed to make his way back to the concert hall. One of the musicians who were performing with me that night recognised him and alerted security. He was taken away again.

The next incident came when I was performing with Il Divo in Berlin. I was walking into the wings at the end of my set when the same man jumped up on stage with a gift of some sort, calling my name and grabbing at me. Fortunately, we had a lot of security people at the side of the stage and he was bundled away very quickly.

It was a shocking experience for me. When I'm up on stage, I consider it to be my space and there's always a line between me and the audience. It's the way I've always been used to things being. As I stand there with my musicians around me, I feel that the stage is a very safe environment on which I can perform without fear. After that horrible occasion, I began to find myself up on stage scanning the audience for the slightest movement. I would notice if somebody five rows back got up to go to the toilet, whereas previously I wouldn't have given it a second thought. It sent real shockwaves through my system.

It has had a negative effect on my career as well, after my management and record company decided that I would no longer tour or release records in Germany for the time being. Everybody at Decca was very understanding and caring towards me; it's one of the occasions when I understood how recording for one of the truly great international record companies is like becoming part of a family. Germany is the biggest classical-music market in Europe and it's frustrating that, as an artist, I simply can't work there at the moment. I'm sad for my genuine fans over there, but, even as I write these words right now, the thought of travelling there makes my stomach turn. It was a very frightening experience, although I'm afraid to say that it's an increasingly common problem for people – and particularly women – in the public eye.

I realise that I'm not alone in facing the problem, but it makes it no easier when you are the victim of this sort of unwanted attention.

CHAPTER 12
TRAVELLING THE WORLD

One of the great privileges of being an international recording artist, as opposed to one who works in only one country, is that I get to travel all over the world. Whenever I tour, I always learn a few phrases in the local dialect, such as 'Nice to meet you – I'm looking forward to working with you.' I also find out how to introduce myself and to say 'please' and 'thank you'.

I always enjoy finding out about each of the different countries and I've become quite a connoisseur of the surprisingly varied cultural sensitivities in each area. I enjoy visiting places such as Hong Kong, Malaysia, Taiwan and South Korea. The culture is so different from what I'm used to either back home in Christchurch or in my adopted home in London. Although nearly all the people I meet speak excellent English, when they revert to their own language I enjoy being in my own little world without a clue as to what they are discussing. Giving interviews in a foreign language is a particularly easygoing experience. First the interviewer asks a question, then the translator translates it. I then answer in English and sit around for a couple of minutes while my answer is translated – and so it goes on, with these little gaps while I just sit there smiling. It's much less hard work than doing an interview in English.

Japan is one of the countries that I've visited most often and I love going there. Japanese fans are more enthusiastic than those from any other nation on earth. They are extraordinarily warm and their generosity knows no bounds. There's a lot of gift giving throughout every trip and I've learned to come prepared with gifts of Kiwi soft toys, New Zealand chocolates and the like.

I've always been intrigued by the Japanese culture and lifestyle. I've read a lot about the importance of the diet that they have there in increasing general levels of health and fitness throughout the population, especially when compared with parts of Europe and America.

As you will have worked out by now, healthy eating is one of my particular fascinations, so I always try to embrace the culinary culture as well as other local customs while I'm there. That means that, every morning I'm in Japan, I always eat a full Japanese breakfast of grilled fish, miso soup, pickles and rice. I absolutely love it and find that it really sets me up for the day in a way that a croissant or a couple of pieces of toast would never do.

However, one particular morning, I learned my lesson when it comes to being too adventurous in the food department. We always stayed in a hotel where there was a choice of a Western breakfast or a traditional Japanese breakfast. I always opted for the latter, but on the day in question I had been up very late performing and had slept in, missing the normal breakfast slots in the restaurant. During the rest of the morning, they offered a more limited menu, which was not quite as good as my normal fare. As I looked at the menu, I vowed that I would try to get up on time in future.

Then I noticed that they were serving Japanese porridge. Now, I like my porridge as much as the next girl and I thought it might be an interesting proposition with a Japanese twist to it. It turned out to be the most revolting thing I've ever tasted before or since. If I had known what to expect, I might conceivably have gained more enjoyment from the meal, although I'm not entirely sure about that.

First, I was served up a bowl of rice porridge, which looks and tastes a lot different from the oat-based porridge that we are used to. The shock came when the condiments were brought to me. I sprinkled them on rather absent-mindedly and took a mouthful. There was an overpowering taste of fish. I looked more closely at the condiments and realised that I was eating little dried baby fish in their entirety, complete with heads, eyes and tails. Now I do eat a bit of fish, but never when you can see their eyes. Whitebait's a big part of many dishes in New Zealand, but I simply can't bear the thought of it. I don't like anything that watches me while I'm eating it. So that taught me a lesson about being too adventurous with food in foreign countries. Maybe I should stick to what I know. Perhaps there's nothing wrong with a piece of toast covered in Vegemite, after all.

On my most recent trip to Japan, I was there to record a commercial for a new range of Bourbon products made from genuine New Zealand boysenberries. It was a major

With the inspiring Ghanian girls that my Bikes for Ghana campaign is supporting

Above: Digging at Alfred Salter School, 2007

Left: Supporting the Women's Environmental Network

With Kofi Anan at the
UN building in New
York . . .

With the Dalai Lama
in Derry . . .

And with Donny
Osmond at the Royal
Variety Performance

Above: Performing with Andrea Bocelli, one of my major influences growing up
Below: A duet with José Carreras, another musical legend

Above: At the New Zealand Music Awards with hip hop group Misfits of Science

Right: Attempting to teach Frank Skinner to sing

Above: Just one perk of the job: in the changing room of the all-conquering All Blacks
Below: With New Zealand prime minister Helen Clark, as Pure went ten-times platinum

Above: With Steve and Giselle on my eighteenth birthday

Left: Signing albums at Cadogan Hall
Below: About to go down the tunnel in Cardiff's Millennium Stadium to sing the New Zealand national anthem

Left: Celebrating my eighteenth birthday with my family in London after they'd flown over to surprise me! **Below:** Isn't my mum a brilliant photographer? She took this photo of me on holiday in New Zealand.

launch, including biscuits, fruit juice, chewing gum and jelly. The Japanese marketplace is an important export zone for New Zealand produce, so I was thrilled when I was asked to promote the products in Japan. Contrary to what some of my friends have suggested, this didn't mean that I recorded a television commercial dressed up as a giant boysenberry, so I'm sorry to disappoint them. I did make a commercial, though, and it was a very Japanese experience.

I arrived in a hotel room with Kathryn, my co-manager. As the door opened, I realised that there were around thirty people in this normal-sized hotel room, all waiting very quietly for my arrival. You name it – they were there: the director, producer, lighting team, cameramen, sound crew, wardrobe, makeup, advertising agency. And they all had assistants. And even some of the assistants had assistants.

Kathryn and I looked at each other in surprise because this was not the actual shoot for the commercial, but just a meeting beforehand. The wardrobe lady presented me with the dresses that they wanted me to wear, and I needed to get changed. That meant that all thirty or so of them had to troop out of the room and into the corridor outside. Then, when I was changed, all thirty of them filed back in, looked me up and down, smiled encouragingly and voiced their approval.

When it came to filming, there were even more people involved. The production team were very conscious that I should take breaks. These would last for one minute each while I sat in a chair with people fanning me and holding my water. It was ridiculous because in each of the breaks hordes of people were brought up to be presented to me. In the end, I had to escape to the loos just to get a breather because there were people fussing around me the whole time.

Once everything had finished, I realised how big a deal it was for everybody there. Apparently, the commercial is on all the time and it uses my track 'Summer Rain', which I co-wrote. As you can imagine, I was quite chuffed that they had chosen a song that I had written from the dozens on my albums.

I'm always in awe of how hard Japanese people work and I really appreciate how keen they are to maximise every opportunity for me when I'm there. They always have lots of work lined up for me, which suits me because I would much rather be out meeting and talking to people than sitting on my own in a hotel room.

While we were in Japan making the commercial, we stayed in a different hotel from normal. Unusually, I had a day off after arriving there and I suggested to Kathryn that we go for a swim in the hotel pool. She was too tired and wanted to sleep, but I was full of energy and was determined to burn some of it off with a swim. This was going to prove to be a more difficult prospect than I had imagined.

I walked towards the hotel spa and then discovered that I had left my goggles in my room, so I had to walk back upstairs to get them. After this false start, I went back to the health spa and finally managed to locate the swimming pool area in the huge hotel complex.

I was a little confused about how everything worked and I had a suspicion that there would be a certain amount of etiquette, as is common in Japanese life. I was given a key and directed down a corridor by the lady behind the desk. This is going to be easy, I thought, as I walked through the door into the middle of a gym class. Flushing bright red, I backed out of the room and tried the next door along. By this stage, my stress levels were starting to rise, as I was unsure about what to expect, kind of defeating the purpose of the swim in the first place.

I finally found the correct door. As I walked through it, I noticed a sign that read PLEASE TAKE OFF YOUR SHOES. I looked around and saw a few rows of shoes placed neatly on a mat in front of me. Next to them were rows of little slippers with the word Spa emblazoned across the front. I assumed that guests were supposed to take off their outdoor shoes and put on the slippers instead. It seemed to make sense. I put on a pair of the spa slippers and walked through the door on the other side of the changing room.

Suddenly, a lady appeared from nowhere and screamed at me while gesticulating wildly at my feet and simultaneously shooing me back through the door. It was obvious that wearing the spa slippers in that area was not the done thing.

I stood in the changing room and looked around. There were lockers all down one wall. I was unsure about where to go next, but I had been given a key with a number and I knew that it must match up to one of the lockers. I was already wearing my bikini underneath my gym gear, so I just needed somewhere to leave my outer garments. I walked into one area and all of the women there gave me a very strange look and pointed in another direction. So I realised that I was not supposed to be heading for those lockers.

Nobody spoke English and I realised quite how easy life usually is for us English speakers in foreign countries. Because so many people generally do speak our language, we come to expect others to make the effort. This situation caught me by surprise and I wished I had brought along my Japanese phrase book, which I had travelled with on my first few visits.

Eventually, I found a lady who worked in the spa. Through a mixture of signing and the odd English word, she showed me to my locker and handed me a robe and a towel. I was not too certain about anything at this stage, but I assumed that now was the time for me to get changed. I hung my gym gear up in the locker and attached the key to my wrist. Wearing the robe and carrying the towel, I set off for the water. At the same time, I hoped that I had changed in the place where I was supposed to change and that I was not supposed to be somewhere else. I was very mindful of the fact that Japanese people are quite modest, with a very definite way of doing things in their polite society.

At this point, I did start to wonder why I was putting myself through this. Perhaps it would have been simpler to have followed Kathryn's example and to have gone for a couple of hours' sleep instead. I still had to find my way to the pool. In front of me, there were a number of different doors with no signs in English. But, then again, I was probably the only crazy enough Westerner who had ever ventured this far into the spa.

I plucked up the courage to walk out through one of the doors. Eventually, after wandering around aimlessly while trying to look as if I knew where I was going, I found the pool. Of course, I *always* made sure that I strode forward in a purposeful manner as if I knew where I was going, because the last thing I wanted anyone to think was that I was a tourist who didn't have a clue about what to do. One of my instincts when travelling is to avoid behaving like a tourist – I like to blend in with the locals.

Beside the pool was a control tower with an office at the top looking down on the water beneath. A woman walked out of the office and started to make the internationally recognised sign for 'No' with her hands. I was confused. Why could I not use the pool? She pointed to a book that listed times and names. She spoke a little broken English and I managed to work out that only four people were allowed in the pool at any one time and that they were fully booked at that moment. I had to write down my name in the next available slot, which was half an hour away.

Great! I thought. What am I going to do for half an hour? I just want to get to the pool!

The woman told me that I could use the Jacuzzi in the meantime. As I set off, she realised that I had not showered first. This was not something that I had come across in New Zealand or the UK. She came running down the steps towards me and literally dragged me back to the showers, gesticulating wildly at them. I felt very embarrassed. It was as if my personal-hygiene regime had been called into question.

After my shower, I was allowed into the Jacuzzi, where I sat down, thinking, Thank goodness for that! I had twenty minutes in the steaming water, getting hotter and hotter and wishing against all the odds that someone would get out of the pool early. I watched an elderly couple doing their interminable water aerobics workout in the pool where I should have been. Eventually, one of the swimmers left and it was my turn. Just as I was about to get in, the lady ran down to me again with a hair cap. She looked mortified that I would even *consider* getting into the pool without a hair cap. She shoved it tightly on to my head. I'm not sure which of us was more puzzled by the other's actions.

After all of my battles to get there, I was determined to enjoy my swim. I really wanted to make the most of it, but, by this stage, my skin was starting to shrivel up because I had spent so long in the Jacuzzi.

I climbed out of the pool, after spending a good few extra minutes watching everyone else getting out, just to see what was expected of you after you left the water. I very tentatively turned on a nearby shower, while desperately looking around me for a sign of what normal behaviour would be defined as at this point. There were more towels and more robes neatly folded nearby. With two colours to choose from, I picked the pink robe, guessing that it must be the female one.

I walked back out through the gym area and into the changing rooms. I noticed some baths in the middle of the room, surrounded by Japanese women walking around in the nude without a care in the world. There were also seats around the edge, where other women were sitting applying moisturiser and their makeup. Everything was very neat, very precise.

As I walked further along, I noticed a set of showering booths with stools inside. I felt that taking a bath might be an etiquette minefield and these showers seemed a much safer option. So, even though I had already showered, I took a second shower. I dried myself and changed into my gym clothes. I was probably in the wrong area, but by now, I was beyond caring. I was on the home straight.

I rushed out of the spa and back up to my room feeling that I had achieved something that was so monumental that it was almost worth adding to my CV. A lesser girl would undoubtedly have crumbled and given up far, far earlier. When I regaled Kathryn with my tale of adventure later that evening, she found it hilarious, but must have been quietly glad that she had opted for the nap.

Alongside Japan, America is another of the countries where I've spent a good deal of time over the past couple of years. Breaking America is the holy grail for any recording artist, and managers tend to spend a lot of their waking hours looking for opportunities to perform in front of American audiences.

I first saw the group Celtic Woman on the PBS television channel while I was touring the States with Il Divo. With four attractive female singers and one attractive female fiddle player all aged between eighteen and thirty, they were quickly becoming a huge phenomenon. If you like, they were doing for voice what the musical *Lord of the Dance* did for Irish dance.

A few months later, the team behind the group approached my management and asked whether I would perform as a guest on another PBS television special that they were recording and then join them on their tour of America. I leaped at the opportunity, which sounded fantastic. It felt as if it would be a good springboard for me in the USA and I was excited about the idea of joining a group and having a different experience. I'm always keen to try out new ways of working and, as somebody who has always performed as a solo artist, I was intrigued about the dynamics of working in a group.

I met the Celtic Woman girls for the first time at a lunch in Dublin. I was worried that they might feel that I was muscling in on them after they had done all of the hard work, but I needn't have been concerned, since they were all lovely – very friendly and welcoming, as I've always found Irish people to be. Our lunch was scheduled for the rather strange time of four o'clock in the afternoon. Each of the girls had steak and chips, but, not really being a meat eater, I opted for the fish and chips instead. I hit it off with them instantly and they obviously had a great rapport with each other. We talked about the television show and the plans for the American tour. I left Dublin very excited about working with them.

Soon afterwards, I was back in Dublin for the rehearsals. I quickly realised that, when you're working with a group of other people, you need to know exactly what everyone else is going to do, sing and say at all times, so that you can respond accordingly. We had lots of choreography re-hearsals and, for a brief moment, I was reminded of the time when my sister, our next-door neighbours and I all dressed up as the Spice Girls. This was fun!

Now, I don't want to exaggerate the choreography part of things because there were no dances as such. Instead, there were a lot of occasions when we move around stage, with a few skipping moves thrown in. This was all a very new experience for me in my adult career, although the work that I had done when I was very young and appearing in musicals stood me in good stead. I was very conscious of not mucking things up for the group. As they had all worked together before, I think that it all came more instinctively for them than it did for me. I was very aware that I was playing as part of a team and I wanted to make sure that everything was right so that I wouldn't ruin the show for everyone else.

I loved the music, which is highly energetic and a big change from what I'm used to. I found that I was really in my element standing on the stage and tapping my toe to it. It was heavily amplified and, with the girls all singing, the band playing and a chorus joining in as well, it all made for an infectiously powerful sound.

Ireland and all things Irish are very popular in the States and the television special was recorded at the beautiful Slane Castle in front of an invited audience. The castle is a great venue and has hosted some big rock and pop events in its time with concerts by everyone from U2 to Robbie Williams. The PBS concert was nerve-racking for me. At the outset it was a little strange, because all the other girls lived in Dublin and I was staying in a hotel near to the venue. So, at the end of the rehearsals, they all went home to their families and I went back on my own to the hotel. Despite their friendliness, I still felt quite the outsider.

Everything was fairly last-minute as we prepared to record the televised concert. I started to worry about the costumes. There are only so many times that someone can be told, 'You'll be grand.' It's a nice little phrase, but it doesn't really mean much and was no comfort whatsoever.

There was a lot of new material for me to learn for the ensemble tracks. My solo songs were 'Lascia Ch'io Piangia' and 'Scarborough Fair', both of which appeared on *Odyssey* and posed no problem for me at all. But, with the group songs, I had to remember my harmonies and my lines. Unlike in a solo performance, where I sing every line of every song, I also had to remember the lines where I had to stay silent because it was somebody else's turn to sing. I also had to learn a song in Gaelic, which was a language I've never sung in before, but, after mastering the Welsh national anthem in Welsh, I felt ready for another language.

On the day the Slane Castle concert was being recorded, our second-half costumes were still being finished off. In the first half, we all wore shades of white and blue, while in the latter part of the show we wore rather more fiery colours. My dress was gold. The set was very dramatic with lots of dry ice cascading off the front of the stage, and striking lighting effects and pyrotechnics at the end. We filmed the show over two nights, but it rained on the first night and the orchestra kept having to run off stage to ensure that their instruments stayed dry.

The programme was broadcast in the USA ahead of our tour and I quickly realised when I got there that it had been extremely widely viewed. My first show was in Boston and then it was on to the world-famous Radio City Music Hall in New York. It was only when I arrived in America that I also realised just how major a production it all was. Ranked the seventh biggest tour in the USA during 2007, it used four tour buses that snaked their way from state to state: one for us girls, one for the choir, one for the band and one for the crew. We had a lot of consecutive shows and this made the trip demanding for everyone.

I learned a lot on the tour and I used in-ear monitors for the first time. These are the earpieces that you might have seen singers using during concerts. It allows them to hear exactly what is going on above the background noise. I've always avoided them before, preferring to have wedges at the front of the stage. These are speakers that point in my direction so that I can hear how everything sounds. If any singer has to rely solely on the speakers that are pointing away from them towards the audience, it can be very hard for them to hear their voice and musical accompaniment clearly.

I had tried using in-ears myself only once before, when I was recording my own PBS special in Wellington in 2004. I had found it a very uncomfortable experience and, at the last minute, I asked for monitors to be placed on the front of the stage for me. That was never an option on the Celtic Woman tour because there were five of us performing on stage and each of us needed to be able to hear the other four clearly so that we could harmonise and perform in time with each other.

The benefit of in-ears is the consistency it brings to you. Wherever you perform, no matter what the size of the arena or your position on stage, you always hear a perfect mix of your voice and the music in your ears. But, for me, the drawback is that they made me feel very cut off from the audience. We had a range of different-sized venues on the tour: sometimes we were in stadiums and on other occasions in theatres. I found it very hard that the in-ear monitors removed any sense of scale from the venue. It was also hard to make a connection to the audience in the smaller theatres when they were so close to me and yet I felt cut off in my own little sound bubble.

I love to share the sounds that the audience are hearing, but with in-ears I find myself in a completely different world. So, as a compromise, I used only one of the earpieces on the tour. That meant I could still hear the other girls clearly in one ear, but I could also hear the audience and the venue's natural ambience in the other.

The idea of travelling across America on a tour bus sounds great in theory, but let me tell you, it's very hard work in practice. We usually clambered on to the bus at about 11 p.m. at the end of the show. The next hour or so we would spend chatting and eating. This was a change for me because I usually eat before rather than after concerts. Then we would each climb wearily into our bunks and try to snatch a few hours' sleep before arriving at a hotel in the next city where we were performing, at about 4 a.m. The tour manager would wake us up and we would trundle bleary-eyed off the bus and stagger to our rooms in a zombie-like state before slumping back to sleep.

The girls were all great fun and there was a genuine spirit of camaraderie, not just among the main singers but also among the choir, the band and the production people, nearly all of whom were Irish. The girls introduced me to the delights of American cuisine, a subject they had become experts in after spending the previous couple of years touring the States. There was Irish food on the menu, too, which was brought over by family members on their visits. I was introduced to chocolate mini-eggs, which were the regular after-show treat for the girls, as well as all kinds of cheeses, including Black Diamond Cheddar Cheese, or Extra Sharp Canadian Cheddar, as it's also known. In return, I tried to impart some of my own food knowledge to the girls. Much to my delight, Mairead took to the tamari-toasted almonds, but the goji berries didn't really go down so well.

The girls enjoyed messing around, as I discovered to my cost on stage. At the very end of the performance we would all sing a song called 'Spanish Lady' as our final encore. One of the girls whacked me on the bum as she walked past me in the final piece of choreography. I nearly screamed with surprise. It then became a nightly event and they realised that, even though I knew it was coming, it never failed to surprise me. Finally, one night towards the end of the tour, I managed to guess that I was about to get a simultaneous double whack from two of them and I grabbed their hands before they could make contact. This only made them start laughing. I found that I was quite easily distracted on stage and I struggled to sing through the number without getting a fit of the giggles myself.

I hate being told off and there were two occasions on the tour when I got myself into trouble – both times because I was late for the tour bus. Every day, we were given a call sheet and I found out very quickly that, when it said 'Departure 3 p.m.', it actually *meant* that we would leave at three o'clock on the dot and not a moment later. It was a sensible rule because there were so many people on the tour and, if there was too relaxed an attitude to timekeeping, we would never have left at all. Everyone had to be on time to keep the show literally on the road. The first time I was late, I was let off, but on the second occasion I received a stern talking-to from the tour manager.

In my defence, while everyone else had been asleep, I had been appearing on the wonderfully named breakfast television show *Good Things Utah*. I was tired and so I went back to sleep when I got back to the hotel after the interview. I woke up late and I knew instantly that I wouldn't be on time for the bus. I just hoped that somebody else would be later than I was.

Of course, all the rest had been on time and were sitting in the buses waiting for me. I felt pretty fed up. The last thing I wanted everyone else to think was that I didn't care. Kathryn is the person in my management team whom I always call first when I have this sort of problem, so I rang her to tell her about it. I was embarrassed that I had held everyone up. In reality, I'm not sure that the rest of the production were in the slightest bit bothered, but I still felt guilty for the entire day and I made sure that I turned up early to the bus every day from then onwards.

There was one stage in the tour when I became quite miserable. Although I had felt homesick before when I travelled to London, I always had my family and my management with me. I became sick for a few days with a really sore throat during the tour. While I was feeling under the weather, it felt as if everything was getting on top of me. There was so much going on and so many commitments surrounding the tour that, basically, I couldn't see the light at the end of the tunnel. I couldn't imagine how I could possibly get through it. There was a moment when I felt like getting on a plane and saying, 'You know what? I can't be bothered with all this.'

But it quickly passed as my throat cleared up and I gained a better sense of perspective. One of my best coping mechanisms remains a telephone call home to my family. It's never easy getting hold of them, with the time difference usually forcing one of us to stay up late, but it's so important that we do stay in touch – not just to me, but to the whole family. Mum and Dad are great people to talk to and they are very good at calming me down or putting things into perspective. Whenever I'm on the phone to them, it always lasts for at least an hour. Luckily, they have discovered a cheap phone deal back home, so I usually arrange for them to call me.

Other than when I felt ill, the Celtic Woman tour was a great experience. I know that I learned so much on the tour that will help me later down the track. It pushed me out of my comfort zone and made me do something different. It was quite weird to come back to London and to perform in entire concerts on my own afterwards, although it has given me a renewed appreciation of this way of working.

While I was in America, I really developed as a performer and a person and I also got to know the American people and I feel completely at home in front of American audiences now. They are very enthusiastic and receptive, giving me an extremely positive response wherever I went.

CHAPTER 13
HOW TO DO IT YOURSELF

Having a successful career as a recording artist and as a live concert performer was always the dream for me. There's no reason why it should be unattainable for anyone else, although the journey towards having a hit record or a sell-out concert tour is by no means an easy one. I'm often asked – particularly by the parents or grandparents of young girls aged between twelve and sixteen – what they should do to help their daughters and granddaughters along the way.

The first thing to stress is that there's absolutely no certainty of success and, for every one person for whom the dream does come true, there are thousands of others who discover that it's not their destiny. There are also no absolute rules in this business: what works for one person may prove to be a disaster for another. What I can do, however, is share with you some of the observations I've made along the way.

The very first thing that you have got to have is **talent**. I watch some of the talent competitions that have become so popular around the world and I find myself agreeing with the judges. You have got to have a basis of natural talent. People who think they can take singing lessons to turn a complete inability to sing into a world-class level of singing are deluded.

It's quite all right to take lessons to help improve your singing, but, no matter how good your teacher, you will not become an overnight sensation if you have absolutely no ability to hit the notes in the first place. It simply does not work like that. You have to be born with an instrument that can be fine-tuned by a teacher. It's perfectly possible to develop it in a disciplined way – but you do need an aptitude for music. You must be musically inclined.

To get to a stage where you are making your career out of music for the long term, you don't just need talent, you need significantly *above-average* talent. It's more than just a technical ability to be able to put the right notes in the right place. It really does have to be a **passion**. Even when I was very young, I had that passion for singing.

I realised that people commented on my voice when they heard it. The feedback was so positive and so often that it became obvious that there were not too many people out there who could sing as I could. In a way, my decision to take it further was a very rational rather than emotional one. There are lots of things that I'm not very good at, but I thought to myself, 'OK, singing it is, then. This is what I'm here for; this is what I can offer the world.'

One of the most important factors for a child singer is their **parents**. I'm really grateful that my parents let me try all sorts of different fields, so that I could be sure that the path I wanted to take was the right one. They allowed me to take dancing lessons, to try out sports such as tennis, just in case I discovered that I had a passion or a talent for something that I had not previously considered.

So, although I realise that I've not had any children myself yet, my advice to a parent comes from the child's point of view. You just have to let your child explore different fields. Then, hopefully, the child will be drawn to one field, and that is then the point at which you give them the utmost support to enable them to follow their dream.

You do have to create an environment in which they have space to develop on their own, while at the same time always being there for them when they need support. Remember that children develop talent at different speeds, so don't give up too soon. At the same time, don't push them too hard in one particular direction because that could just put them off altogether.

Desire is a very important asset for any performer. Your child must actually want to become a performer. I've seen cases where one or both parents are living out *their* dreams through their child, who is not anywhere near as keen on the whole thing.

You hear of tennis players who start learning tennis at the age of three. It may be in their blood to be great tennis players, but they end up being put off the sport altogether because their parents have ramrodded them down one defined route. Children must ask themselves, 'How do I know if tennis playing is really something I want to do and that it's not just something that I've been forced into?'

So, you have to allow the child to choose the particular field that they want to be working in and allow them to try different things so that they can be drawn towards one field rather than another, based on an informed decision that they are making themselves.

Dame Malvina Major was a wonderful inspiration and support to me during the period when she was giving me singing lessons. She gave me probably the single most important piece of advice that I've been given before or since: **stay true to yourself**. It's so important because, if you try to be something that you are not or to venture into something that you are not really comfortable with, people will pick up on it very quickly.

For example, if I was to record an album of pop/disco tracks, I would know in the back of my mind that I was doing something that others could probably do better and with more conviction. I don't feel comfortable in that world and I don't think that I would enjoy the idea of a career that is very image-driven and dependent on radio airplay and raunchy videos. I think that, if I did release a record like that, I would fall flat on my face because the public would pick up on my discomfort. They would know that it was not really me, whereas what I'm doing now is very much true to myself. However, who knows how I'll feel a few years down the road? Maybe I'll discover a hidden disco diva inside me!

There are things that you need to be prepared to give up to build a serious music career: heavy partying, for example. Just recently, I'm learning to be a little bit more relaxed about life in general. For so long, I've been so focused and I've not wanted to let anything get in my way to distract me. It's vital to maintain **discipline** as a singer, though.

On the day of a performance, I can be quite precious about my voice. I take all of my live performances very seriously and every time I perform I want to be at my very best. You never know if someone is going to be seeing you for the first time and will be framing their judgement of you as an artist on that performance alone. There's always going to be a new member of the audience at every concert that you give, so going out and partying the night before and having a tired voice is simply not an option.

I'm really pleased that England has now caught up with the rest of the UK in adopting the smoking ban in public places, because there's nothing that plays more havoc with a singer's voice than sitting in a smoky environment.

The old adage says that **practice** makes perfect, and this is another big area for any budding musician. For quite a while, I have to admit that I didn't do much singing practice, but nowadays I try to do around an hour a day. Generally, with singing, there's no need to do hours and hours of practice, but I always make sure that I do my vocal exercises very thoroughly.

There's a fine line to be drawn between enough practice and pushing it too far. It's a tricky one to get right because, when you're on a fully fledged tour, you could be performing every day for at least an hour, *and* you have your vocal exercises and the sound check on top. That's a lot of singing, so you have no time to do anything else with your voice, especially if you are doing a run of consecutive shows.

It's always important to make time in your schedule to work on new material and to **develop your voice**. Scales and exercises are essential, as well as not being afraid to play around with different sounds. That said, you should avoid making sounds that strain the voice and be aware that, although it's good to be physically tired after singing, you should never be vocally tired.

It's impossible to underestimate the importance of the **songs** that you choose to sing. If you will excuse the musical pun, they are absolutely key. It's really important that you be very comfortable with every song that you sing in public. If you are worried about a part of a song, then you are not going to be able to deliver it properly to the audience. I know that the songs that I perform best are the ones that I'm not in any way concerned about singing. I know them back to front and I know that they are in the right key for me. All singers do have notes that are, shall we say, not their favourites. But I'm not going to tell you what mine are, in case you listen out for them when you next hear me sing.

You do need to keep on **learning**. For me, singing in *West Side Story*, which I write about in more detail in the next chapter, was a great opportunity to learn something new. There's a great variety of different styles, moods and emotions wrapped up in the score and it's the first time I've had the opportunity to perform in such an expressive way over such a concentrated period of time.

When I first began singing, I simply enjoyed the act and process of making a nice, tuneful sound and I didn't really have a lot to say. I certainly didn't pay anywhere near as much attention to the lyrics as I do now. As I gain more life experience, I suddenly listen to songs and think to myself, Oh, *now* I understand what this song means. It's even the case with some of the songs that I sang when I was younger, and I sometimes wish that I had understood more when I regularly performed them.

But, when you're just fourteen or fifteen years old, you don't have much experience of life and you don't necessarily have a lot to say about how you feel. So, I'm now really enjoying expressing myself through my song choices and using my own experiences to better help me tell the stories.

As I mentioned earlier, I've been doing some songwriting recently and I've found that my fans have taken really well to songs such as 'Let Me Lie', the first track on my album *Treasure*. I think this is because it's another example of my being true to myself. When I sing 'Let Me Lie', it's a particularly special experience for me because people are hearing my own words and music. Writing lyrics gives me the opportunity to express myself that bit more and, when I sing my own songs, the performance comes from the heart because I'm very connected to them.

One of the hottest areas for me is ensuring that I stay **healthy**. Some people even think I err on the side of freakishness on the subject, but I really do believe that it's so important for a performer. One of my fellow singers on the Celtic Women tour said to me afterwards, 'You've had such a positive influence on me. I've been eating so much more healthily since.'

Mum has always been interested in nutrition, so I've always eaten a healthy **diet** – even as a child. There are plenty of easy little things you can do to help, such as eating wholemeal rather than white bread. When I was younger, I used to find that I would get sick a couple of days before any big performance, usually with a sore throat, which would then develop into a chest infection. I started to take a keen interest in what sorts of things I should be eating to help build up my immune system and to help me become less susceptible to coughs and colds. After extensive research on the Internet and at the library, I began to understand the benefits of eating a diet rich in vitamins and minerals – particularly vitamin C, vitamin A, zinc and selenium.

So now, when I travel and, as almost always happens, when I'm stopped at customs, my bags contain all sorts of health-enhancing pots and potions. I'm a big believer in eating a varied diet, but always try to make sure I get my daily dose of fresh fruit and vegetables, which can be a bit of a mission sometimes when you are reliant on hotel menus and airport cafés.

I try to remember to pack in my suitcase a jar of Marmite, since it's full of useful B vitamins, and alongside that I always take a multivitamin pill and extra vitamin C. I also take some omega-3-rich fish-oil capsules now and then, because we tend not to get enough of this beneficial fat in our diet.

These are what I've found are right for me. I'm in no way suggesting that they would necessarily be right for you, so please do consult a doctor or a nutritionist before you go loading up on supplements, because you can take all of the pills and capsules in the world, but at the end of the day, you need to have a good diet.

I try to eat as much fresh food as possible and to avoid deep-fried and overly processed food. However, I do have to confess one terrible weakness: I absolutely adore airline food. I know that it's often prepackaged and processed, but there's something about it that I just find strangely appealing. You can't be good all the time!

Everybody needs to put aside some time to **rest**. You need to be able to take time out and to understand that you can take a break without your entire career falling to pieces. I have to admit that I've been scared to take time off until recently, because I thought that, if I took a break, I would be missing out on something. But life is not a race and sometimes this is something that I can forget. There's no need to be constantly charging around. Breaks do help to give you a chance to reflect, so that, when you do go back to work, you have a clearer head and better judgement.

I was lucky that my parents managed me themselves until the release of my first international album, *Pure*. It's vitally important, when you do get to the stage when you need a full-time professional **manager**, which is not necessarily right at the beginning of your career, that you find somebody who is on the same page as you and that they don't have a totally different idea of where you should be heading.

I'm really lucky to have worked with Steve Abbott from Bedlam Management since before the release of *Pure*. He has been with me all the way along the journey since then and together we have a clear idea of where we would like my career to go in the future. I owe him a lot. I'm also very lucky that more recently Kathryn Nash has joined Steve in working with me and she's very quickly become a friend as well as part of my management team.

Steve and Kathryn, along with Nicola and Erica, who work with them, form part of my support system. My family are my biggest supporters, though – especially Mum. She gives me an honest opinion every time, and she will never tell me something just to keep me happy. There's always a danger that people will just tell an artist, 'Yeah, it'll be fine. It'll be great.' But Mum will say, 'I don't like that. I do like this.' She's also quite a good reflection of the general public's reaction because she comes at everything from the perspective of a layperson rather than a music professional.

So, I have my family and then a great management team. They are a team that I really do trust. I've worked with Steve for a long time and I feel as if we are all in it together. Whenever we do things, it's a team effort, as opposed to their telling me what to do, or my telling them what to do. I'm also very lucky because Steve and Kathryn are very dedicated to their work. It would be hard to work with a manager who regarded their job as simply a nine-to-five activity. You will never hear Steve or Kathryn say the words, 'Well, I finish at six and that's me done for the day.'

I'm very much a believer in listening to everyone and taking on board their **advice**, to help me come to a decision, which will often be a mixture of what different people have told me. I deal with my voice in the same way. I'll go along to different singing teachers and have lessons with various people and sometimes their advice can be conflicting.

At the end of the day, I'll do whatever feels most comfortable for me. There are so many different ideas and opinions out there that you need to be sure of what you want rather than try to do what other people want – especially when it comes to making an album with your name and picture on the front. If you try to keep all of the experts happy, you are just going to fall flat on your face, because, when it comes to making music, the whole thing is so subjective. It's very hard to manufacture a hit album –

they tend to come about in a far more organic way. For example, anyone trying slavishly to recreate *Pure* today would struggle. There's no point in one artist simply mimicking a format that has been successful for another artist. It's almost inevitable that direct copycats don't work out as well as the original artist. So, it's important to follow your gut instincts. Even if your album is not as successful as you would have liked, you will have been true to yourself and you will have created something of which you can be proud. It also means that you can't blame anyone else if it goes wrong.

It can be quite a lonely existence, particularly when you are travelling around the world, so you do have to be quite **independent**. Some people cope with this by employing a huge entourage to travel with them. I quite like my own space and having some peace and quiet before a performance, so the last thing that I would want would be a room full of people.

The artists with big entourages tend to forget that they are actually paying for all these hangers-on to be around them. They are not necessarily their friends: they are their employees. If they arrive somewhere with half a dozen hair-stylists, makeup artists and dressers, these people are all being paid by somebody – and it's usually ultimately the artists themselves, although the record company may pick up the initial bill, before charging it back against income that has yet to be earned by the artist through selling records. I would much rather remember my roots and keep it real.

When you spend half of your time travelling and waiting in queues to go through security, **patience** is an important virtue. It becomes even more significant when you discover that you have been randomly selected for a baggage search yet again. When it comes to your career, you don't want to be *too* patient, though. You should never rest on your laurels and there are times when it pays to be snapping at people's heels to make things happen.

You need to have a healthy amount of hunger and self-reliance. You can't always rely on other people to remember to do things for you. On some occasions, there's simply no substitute for doing something yourself, especially if it's important that it really does get done.

When I'm recording, I'm especially keen to ensure that we end up with the best possible track. It's dangerous if the people around you become too laid back about making records. The one problem that most artists face is that people get so caught up in image and all of the dozens of things going on around them that the very reason they are there – the **music** – can be forced to take a back seat if they are not careful, whereas it really should be at the forefront of everything.

If your dream does come true and you finally do get the break that you so desperately want, always remember why you started to perform in the first place and how you have arrived at your goal. For me, I always go back in my mind to my early days in Christchurch and ask myself, 'Which songs really worked for me when I was out busking? Which songs grabbed people's attention? Which songs and what style of singing earned me my record contract?'

I first got noticed because of my pure classical-sounding voice. If I were suddenly to change my tune and do something in the pop style, it would be dangerous. It might work, but it would be a long way from the reason I've got to where I'm today. Record companies can often try to push an artist in a particular direction. My American record company tried to move me towards being a pop artist, but I resisted, saying, 'Wait a minute! I got signed because of my classical music, *not* because I was a pop artist. Now, you're trying to make me pop – something I'm not.'

My final piece of advice to any would-be singer is don't ever forget that doing this job should be **fun**. Life is there to be enjoyed and it can be easy to overlook this as we all get so caught up in chasing after goals. I always have to remind myself that happiness is not a destination, it's a journey. I think it's so important that we should not be constantly chasing after things and that we actually go out and enjoy the moment.

It's very easy to let this pass us by because the world that we live in now is so fast-moving. I try to make sure that, as well as setting myself goals, which I'll hopefully achieve in time, I also live in the present and enjoy that too.

CHAPTER 14
NEW BEGINNINGS

The music industry has a sense of momentum about it. People come and people go; not just those in front of the microphone in the public eye, but those behind the scenes, too. If there's one thing that I've learned over the past four years since *Pure* was released, it's that any successful artist constantly needs to be looking for the next development in their career. Those people who stand still risk getting stuck for ever. So, when Dickon Stainer and Mark Wilkinson at Universal Classics and Jazz in the UK suggested that I might like to consider singing the role of Maria in their new recording of Leonard Bernstein's legendary musical *West Side Story*, celebrating the work's fiftieth anniversary, I jumped at the chance.

The tenor Vittorio Grigolo agreed to sing the leading male role and Maria's love interest, Tony. I was totally into the idea from the start. In terms of age, we are well suited to the parts. We also fit the bill in that we are two different nationalities, with Vittorio coming from Italy. It was one of those offers that I didn't have to think twice about. I've always been a huge fan of the music because it's so varied and, to put it simply, because it's absolutely packed full of really great tunes.

Leonard Bernstein was such a talented guy and his score embraces opera, musical theatre, rock, jazz and pop. He really has it all in there, which could be a complete nightmare on paper, but the way in which he skilfully blends these different influences together creates a sublime musical work.

For me personally, singing Maria was quite a departure from what I've been used to, but I relished the opportunity. It's what I would describe as a 'big sing' and the role is demanding because it covers a lot of ground vocally and emotionally. Maria goes through sadness, anger, excitement and passionate love all in the space of a few songs. As well as different styles of singing, the role covers quite a big range of notes as well. Despite the challenge, I loved singing it and found the whole experience of making the album exhilarating and totally rewarding.

My own links to *West Side Story* go back to when I was very young, when I sang 'I Feel Pretty' at my end-of-year ballet recital, leading the rest of the class in a performance of the song. At that age, not knowing anything about the song's context in terms of the musical as a whole, I felt very vain singing it.

A couple of years later, I saw *West Side Story* in its entirety and gained a much better appreciation of the story.

Gradually, I began to sing more of the songs, such as 'One Hand, One Heart' and 'Tonight'. My favourite song of Maria's is 'I Have a Love', which comes after 'A Boy Like That'. In the song, Maria tells her brother's girlfriend, Anita, that she knows that she should not be in love with Tony because he's not from the same background. Anita has told her that he's wrong for Maria. Maria says that she understand that he's wrong for her in so many ways, but she loves him and there's nothing that she – or anyone else – can do about it.

It's a fantastic part of the story, where the audience has just heard 'A Boy Like That', which is a very intense moment, and then they hear 'I Have a Love', which is more romantic and reflective. It pulls on the audience's heart-strings and I defy anyone not to be moved when they see it performed on stage.

Both Vittorio and I would love to take the roles of Tony and Maria on stage in a full production of *West Side Story*. So far we have sung the full parts together only when we were making the CD. We did perform highlights from the musical at an outdoor Classic FM concert at Woburn Abbey. This was quite an experience, since, even though it was in the height of summer, it came right in the middle of England's biggest flooding crisis in living memory. The wet weather didn't manage to dampen everyone's spirits, though, and it was very much a typically English occasion.

I'm full of admiration for performers who appear in long runs of musicals. Actors who appear in musical theatre are incredibly talented and have enormous stamina, and I like to think that it's something that I could imagine myself trying out at some stage in my career.

West Side Story came at just the right time for me because, although I found the music pushed me in new directions, it coincided with a natural growth in my voice as I become older. At the moment, I'm really enjoying the new dimensions to my voice and exploring different sensations and different spaces of resonance.

Things can still go wrong, though. I've come to realise that life as a singer is never entirely smooth and sometimes I've only myself to blame. I tend to leave things to the last minute; I hold my hands up and admit that it's one of my many faults. Now, I love my sleep and, as far as I'm concerned, it's not just that I'm lazy. Rest is very important for the voice. I always try to maximise my sleeping time. I can get ready in twenty minutes in the morning, if I have to, and I like to set my alarm for as late as possible.

When I was back in New Zealand at the beginning of 2007, I was asked to sing 'Pokarekare Ana' and 'Abide With Me' on *Good Morning*, the live national breakfast television show. I arrived at the TV station and thought that I had a comfortable hour to sort out my hair and makeup and generally get myself organised. As I walked through the door, one of the producers said to me, 'We'd love to have you on air in ten minutes.' Panic-stricken, I charged into the hair and makeup room and warmed up my voice sitting in the chair while the makeup lady fussed around me.

I knew that I was appearing on the programme twice, in two different segments. I was told that I would be singing my old favourite 'Pokarekare Ana' in the first segment and that 'Abide With Me' would be coming up later on in the morning. This suited me because I was hoping to go over the words to 'Abide With Me', just to refresh myself, since it was a song that I had not performed live for quite some time.

I walked into the studio and tested the microphone during a pre-recorded package just before I was due to go on air. Then the presenters introduced me as singing 'Abide With Me'. I panicked. I should have launched into 'Pokarekare Ana' regardless, but, instead, I thought to myself, Oh sure, I can do this. I know the words.

I was singing *a cappella* and so I had no clues from the musicians as to which words were coming next. I knew the first verse. Things were going fine. As I was coming to the end of the first verse, I realised that I was uncertain of the second verse and I had a choice to make: I could either stop there or I could carry on and try my chances at getting the second verse right. I had a fifty–fifty chance of pulling it off. I decided to go on because I thought that it would be noticeably too short if I sang only the one verse of 'Abide With Me'. Looking back, I realise I should have stuck to the one verse and nobody would have known. But in the heat of the moment – when I asked myself, 'Should I or shouldn't I?' – I took the risk and messed it up.

I started to sing the second verse and then my mind went completely blank. I couldn't remember the second line of the second verse. My heart was pounding; my palms were sweating; my mind was blank. Even though it happened in a split second, thoughts raced through my mind: Oh, my gosh! I've never done this before. I've never forgotten the words to a song live on national TV. Please come to me. Please come to me. I said a little prayer, but it didn't work.

I was convinced that my reputation was about to go down the gurgler. It was not as if I were singing a trite pop song, either: 'Abide With Me' is a hymn with very meaningful words. It's a hymn to which lots of people watching the television that morning knew the correct words. In the end, I made up the rest of the verse. Perhaps every second word was correct. I think some of the words might roughly have had the same vowel sounds as the correct version.

I'm not quite sure how many people realised. I certainly didn't want to highlight it because it seemed that the people around me in the studio had no idea. One of the guests appearing on the programme later on came up to me and said, 'Oh, it was beautiful.' At that point, I decided that maybe I should just keep quiet.

I met up with my friend Emma Ritchie later that day.

'Did you watch me on TV?' I asked tentatively, because I was curious to see what she said.

'Yeah, yeah,' came the nonchalant reply.

'Did you notice anything strange about the lyrics?' piped up Mum, with a cheeky glint in her eye.

Emma paused and said, 'Now that you come to mention it, I was doing my ironing and there was a point when I looked up and thought that there was something strange about the song, but I dismissed it from my mind and carried on with the iron.'

If Emma had not spotted it straightaway, then I was pretty certain that I had got away with it by the skin of my teeth and that my reputation was not in tatters. I'm often asked how I remember the words to so many songs. For one thing, it's my job to know the words and, whereas you might sing along to the words of a song that you hear on the radio or on a CD, unlike me, you are not *paid* to remember the words. Singers develop a huge repertoire of music that they can remember and they tend not to think too hard about the processes they use to commit those words to their memory banks. If you intellectualise it too much, there's a danger that you might start panicking and that this might cause you to forget the words.

I pick up lyrics and tunes through repetition. If I have a piece to learn in a hurry, I listen to it on repeat on a CD or on my iPod. I play it over and over again while I'm doing my chores around the house. If I have a long journey, I take printed scores with me and read through them over and over. Sometimes, it's the old repertoire that can be the most scary because I find that it lulls me into a false sense of security. I like to mix up the song choices in my live concerts with tracks from each of my albums. This means that occasionally I come to sing something that I've performed a million times before, but not for a while, and I'm hit by a moment of realisation that I might not remember the words.

Thankfully, though, they do seem to be indelibly etched on to my brain on all occasions – except for appearances on early-morning breakfast television shows!

CHAPTER 15
LOOKING BACK AND LOOKING FORWARD

I'm going to begin this final chapter by writing about something that I touched upon in the very first chapter, when I told you the story of my pride at performing the New Zealand national anthem on the pitch of the Millennium Stadium in Cardiff, ahead of the All Blacks' match against Wales.

In a similar way, I was particularly proud at the beginning of 2007 to be asked to sing at the ANZAC Day Memorial

Service, which happens at six o'clock in the morning. It was a huge honour to sing in front of the veterans both at the service and afterwards at a local *marae* (a Maori meeting house). As we drank coffee laced with a drop of rum and munched on divine Anzac biscuits, I reflected on the bond I have with my homeland, which has done nothing but strengthen since I've started to spend the majority of my time in other parts of the world. It was a very special day for me and, whenever I'm singing a song on behalf of my fellow New Zealanders, I do become very emotional. And unashamedly so.

On my first stay in London when I was fifteen, I pined for New Zealand; my family and friends; the country that I had grown up with. I felt quite the foreigner amid the hustle and bustle of London's busy roads, where there's constant movement and energy. I've grown to love London now, but being away has made me appreciate the wide, empty streets of Christchurch and the sheer amount of space that we are all able to enjoy in New Zealand.

I missed out on going on the normal OE, or overseas experience. It's a real rite of passage for young Kiwis, after school or university, to take a year out travelling to different parts of the world. Fiona Pears, the violinist who usually performs with me, alongside my musical director and pianist Ian Tilley, is another Kiwi from Christchurch who is living in London. She often talks about her big OE backpacking around Europe and about all the friends she made while doing it. Sometimes, I think to myself how amazing it would be if I disappeared with a rucksack and travelled across France, Spain and Italy. It sounds absolutely amazing, but I'm not sure that it will be something that I'll ever get around to, because I enjoy my work so much. I certainly don't feel that I've missed out because I've worked; I've just done things in a different way from usual. Arguably, I've spent the past five years on the biggest OE that any Kiwi has ever had.

After the success of *Pure*, when I was still only sixteen or seventeen, I guess that I was not quite so aware of how lucky I was. It's only just now that I'm realising how harsh the world is and how cutthroat life can be. To have an opportunity like this is just incredible and I feel very fortunate to be in this situation. My hobby is my job and my job is my hobby.

If I took time out to backpack around Europe, I would miss my work. I've mentioned in earlier chapters that I'm quite a focused person, so I suspect that I would spend the whole trip wondering what I should be doing to further my singing career. It's important to me and I've always wanted to be a singer from as early as I can remember.

I was quite shy as a child, but I was quietly driven. I've always been that way. Even my parents were sometimes quite surprised when I showed my drive. These days, though, they have a better picture of who I am. I guess that I still come across as quite a laid-back person and I put a lot of that down to my upbringing in New Zealand.

I'm aware that having a star in the family has not always been easy for everyone. To a certain extent, my brother and sister have had to grow up with a big sister whom everybody knows and talks about. I think the hardest part for them was when I was aged between fourteen and seventeen. Those few years must have been really tough on Sophie and Isaac because Mum and Dad spent a lot of their time touring with me as I went off around the world for the first time. There was also a lot of media attention and they had to put up with 'Hayley this' and 'Hayley that' or 'I saw Hayley on this show' at every turn. For that reason, I think it has been great over the past couple of years that Mum and Dad have been at home looking after them, while I've been away doing my own thing. I would still like to be there more often to be a big sister, especially to Sophie. I miss doing the regular girly things that sisters take for granted.

I did need to spread my wings, though. As I grew older, I became more independent and less reliant on Mum and Dad. In the end, they told me that they started to feel like spare wheels as they followed me around. They themselves wanted me to start to look after myself. It's a natural part of changing from a child to an adult. It's a tricky thing to get right, though, especially when you're making that change in the public eye. I think that's why, so often, child stars have very public and spectacular fallings-out with their parents, especially when the parent has been operating as a manager as well as a mum or a dad. It always makes for a good story in the newspapers and there have been some very well-publicised instances over the past few years.

That was never the case with the relationship between me and my mum and dad. I found the process very hard. I desperately wanted them to know that I was not just brushing them aside. There was no falling-out and they are still a vital part of what I do. They understand that I'm at an age where I'm capable of looking after myself. They enjoyed the travelling and the sights that they saw around the world. Dad relished the visits to Japan and Mum loved hanging out with me in London. But nowadays they gain more fulfilment by being at home and knowing that they are looking after Sophie and Isaac, who are at an age where they need their mum and dad around them. They are great parents who are there for them night and day, just as they were there for me at that time in my life.

I am still amazed and excited by the opportunities that come my way. Only recently, I flew to Derry and sang in front of the Dalai Lama, which was a huge honour. Richard Moore, a remarkable man, who runs a charity called Children in Crossfire, invited me there. As a young boy in Northern Ireland, he was shot in the eye and blinded by a soldier. When he was older, he decided that he wanted to see the soldier in question and to let him know that he forgave him. It must have taken a lot of courage on both their parts to meet up. The Dalai Lama heard their story and wanted to meet them. I performed 'Pokarekare Ana' and 'Danny Boy' at a special event, held in honour of His Holiness. I was thrilled to shake hands with him and he gave me one of his famous warm smiles. His speech was particularly inspiring and I was struck by the way in which his message crosses all divides. In a much smaller way, I hope that my music also crosses divides.

Going on the Celtic Woman tour has helped to toughen me up. I used to be quite precious if I failed to get my nine hours' sleep every night and to worry that I was therefore going to perform at a level below expectations. I do get quite uptight about following a routine that I'm comfortable with, whereas when I was with Celtic Woman, I had no choice but to be relaxed about the whole thing. At first, after each show, I used to feel that I should get straight to sleep in my bunk on the coach. Then I thought, You know what? Sometimes it's good just to stay up and chat a bit, to be sociable. It taught me that, if I'm a little more relaxed about everything, my work will not automatically suffer.

During the past few weeks, while I've been writing this book, I've realised that the same thing is true about the way in which I separate my work life and my personal life. Until this point, I've been so focused on my work that it has been everything to me. I think that it will always be incredibly important to me because doing a job like this is, to a certain extent, a lifestyle choice and it gives me so much pleasure. But I do need to become better at drawing the line. Sometimes, it's good to go out, to party and to let my hair down. I think that it could actually benefit my work because I'll be slightly more balanced as an individual and less uptight about things. I still have to find that balance and that is something that I'm still working out for myself at the moment.

It does not mean that I'm about to go off the rails and throw all of my self-discipline out of the window. I'll never smoke and I'll never go out drinking alcohol before a gig. But recently I've learned to be a little more relaxed on my days off and I think this has helped to put me in a better frame of mind. It can be quite draining to be constantly focused on work. Sometimes, I feel that I have to try new things to break up the routine. It's interesting that right through my teenage years I've never rebelled. I suppose I was too busy having a fantastic time making records, performing in concerts and meeting new people in different places around the world, to find anything to rebel against. I've always said that I might rebel against something one day, though. And, when it comes, it's going to be spectacular!

There was never a time when I decided to be a singer. Instead, I just followed my voice. I was never entirely sure about what style I wanted to get into, so I tried everything. My ideas have changed from year to year and from album to album. I always knew that I didn't want to concentrate solely on one type of singing and, when I was younger, I actively set out to cross genres. Recently, I've been enjoying discovering different parts of my voice and have started to develop my own personal sound.

As a singer ages and they practise more, their voice acquires more depth. Only recently do I feel that my voice has become more secure and settled – not *completely* settled, but noticeably more so than it was a year ago. That is a very exciting place for me to be, because younger voices can be very fragile instruments. This is not something that is specific to me: all singers go through this gradual change.

Recently, I've found myself starting to enjoy singing more operatic pieces with a truer operatic sound. That is because my voice is feeling more grounded. It has made me think seriously about taking my music in a more operatic direction. But don't hold me to this, because my ideas change constantly. Although opera might come to the fore for a period, I don't think that I ever want to give up singing my other styles.

If someone forced me to define what I do at the moment, I would say that my style of singing is contemporary classical. It's a label I'm very comfortable with. I do like to challenge myself and I do like variety. I definitely don't want to build a career based on the same old handful of songs. Certainly, at times, I do crave a bit of routine, but change and moving forward are important. They are a big part of what I am.

Some people have natural talent and some people have 'learned talent'. I would put myself somewhere in the middle. When it comes to my singing, it has always been a very organic process, where I've followed my natural sound, letting my voice lead the way. But it has definitely helped that I've had violin and piano lessons to teach me how to read music. Any professional singer these days needs to be able to follow a score.

For example, when I'm recording a song for a film soundtrack, I'm usually handed the song for the first time on the day. If you are recording with an orchestra, you need to be able to count the bars. I find myself counting away frantically because I don't want to muck things up in front of all the players. Being able to sight-read music is a necessity rather than a luxury and that is a piece of advice that I would give to anyone who wants a serious career as a professional singer.

I've realised that you do have to be tough in this business and I've become more confident in myself and in my own abilities and opinions. In the record business, you hear of so many people who are dropped and disappear without trace. One minute they are signed; they release an album; the record company get what they want out of them; and then they drop them like a stone. I've come to realise that you have to be tough because the world outside is a tough place.

I was lucky in that I had my opportunity quite young. That meant that I didn't have to go through years of knocking on record companies' doors. My record contract was never handed to me on a silver plate, but, equally, I didn't go through twenty years of rejections, either. Because I achieved what I did at the age that I did, it has taken me a little bit longer to realise how tough the industry is. I've learned that I do need to be a little more ruthless than comes naturally to me. But I'm pretty sure that I've not turned into a heartless person – not yet, at least! When fame hit, my friends stood by me. It's really important for me to have a circle of buddies whom I knew before the moment that my records became successful.

As I come to the end of the final chapter of this book, there are still lots of questions that face me. I don't know where I'm going to end up living permanently. I'm loving London at the moment, but New Zealand is my home. I do intend to do lots more travelling.

Top of my list is Brazil, which I've been promising my best friend, Sophie Brinkers, I'll visit with her for the last few years. How can you possibly have a favourite country until you've seen all of the countries in the world? Music is a bit like that too; it's a journey. A lot of people do their own personal musical exploration out of the public eye. Then, once they have a fix on their place in the landscape, they share it with everyone else on an album. But I've made my musical journey in the public eye and I know that there's so much left for me to discover.

So this is the story, in my own words, of the first twenty years of my life. There's plenty more to come from me and perhaps, in another twenty years' time, I'll sit down to write a second instalment. I've had some amazing experiences already, more than most people pack into an entire lifetime.

I've loved every minute of the roller-coaster ride so far and there's no way that I want to get off.

As I wrote back in the Introduction, all those pages ago, I hope that becoming well known for my singing has not changed me one little bit. I don't think it has. In my mind, I'm still little old Hayley from Christchurch in New Zealand.

I really am just like any other twenty-year-old, except that I've made some albums and have performed in some concerts – and now I seem to have written my very own book as well.

Discography

Many of my albums are released under slightly different covers or names, or with slightly different track listings, in different territories around the world. Rather than listing dozens of marginally varying versions for each of my albums, I've chosen to give you details of the best-selling versions here. There simply is not enough space to list all of them, so, if you have a special edition of one of my albums that is not listed here, then please accept my apologies for its absence from the discography below. I'm still delighted that you bought it – and I hope that you are still enjoying listening to it!

Albums

Walking in the Air

This is my very first album, and was produced by my family in 2000. It was never on general release to the public. I used it as a demo to get my record contract with Universal Music New Zealand.

Tracks
Con te Partiro
La Luna Che Non C'e
Il Mare Calmo della Sera
Another Suitcase in Another Hall
Unexpected Song
Memory
Wishing You Were Somehow Here Again
The Mists of Islay
Walking in the Air
Pie Jesu
How Deep Is Your Love?
Groovy Kind of Love
Eternal Flame

Hayley Westenra

Released by Universal Music, New Zealand in 2001, this is my first professional album. Recorded in around a week, it was the launch pad for everything that has followed for me.

Tracks
Walking in the Air
Ave Maria (J S Bach)
Memory

All I Ask of You
Somewhere
The Mists of Islay
Ave Maria (Schubert)
Bright Eyes
Pie Jesu
Wishing You Were Somehow Here Again
I Dreamed a Dream
Love Changes Everything
God Defend New Zealand
Amazing Grace (Live with the Royal Scots Dragoon Guards)

My Gift to You

This is the follow-up album to my eponymous professional debut. It was released in New Zealand by Universal Music New Zealand in November 2002. As you can see, many of the tracks have a Christmas theme to them. It was the last album that I made for Universal Music New Zealand before I made my first international album for Decca. What was particularly exciting about this album was the fact that my sister Sophie joined me in a couple of the songs.

Tracks
All I Have to Give
You'll Never Walk Alone
Chestnuts Roasting on an Open Fire
Mary Did You Know?
The Peace Song
Do You Hear What I Hear?
Somewhere Over the Rainbow
Gabriel's Message
Pokarekare Ana

Through These Eyes
Morning Has Broken
Silent Night

Pure (UK original edition, Decca, 2003)

This is the album that really started it all for me. Released by Decca in 2003, it became the best-selling debut album in the history of the UK classical charts and the best-selling album of all time by a local artist in New Zealand chart history, going eighteen times platinum.

Tracks
Pokarekare Ana
Never Say Goodbye
Who Painted the Moon Black?
River of Dreams
Benedictus
Hine e Hine
Dark Waltz
Amazing Grace
In Trutina (from *Carmina Burana*)
Beat of Your Heart
Heaven
Wuthering Heights
Hine e Hine (Maori mix)

Bonus CD released in 2004

Tracks
Mary Did You Know?
Bridal Ballad (from the film *The Merchant of Venice*)
Pokarekare Ana (Vocalise)
My Heart and I (from the film *La Piovra*)
Across the Universe of Time

Silent Night, Holy Night
Away in a Manger
Pokarekare Ana (video track)

Wuthering Heights

This 2004 mini-album was released only in Japan.

Tracks
Wuthering Heights (new version)
Pokarekare Ana (new version)
Hine e Hine (acoustic version)
Away in a Manger
Never Say Goodbye

Odyssey (original edition, Decca, 2005)

My second album for Decca sees me spreading my wings musically. I was still on my musical journey when I recorded this, hence the title. It includes the first track that I co-wrote for one of my albums, 'What You Never Know (Won't Hurt You)'.

Tracks
Prayer
Dell'amore Non Si Sa
Never Saw Blue
Ave Maria (Caccini)
What You Never Know (Won't Hurt You)
Quanta Qualia
Both Sides Now
May It Be
Bachianas Brasilieras No. 5 Aria
Bridal Ballad

The Mists of Islay
O Mio Babbino Caro
Laudate Dominum
Wiegenlied
She Moves Through the Fair
Dido's Lament

Odyssey (special edition, Decca, 2006)

Tracks
May It Be
The Water Is Wide
Dell'amore Non Si Sa (duet with Andrea Bocelli)
Lascia Ch'io Pianga
Prayer
Ave Maria (Caccini)
Scarborough Fair
Quanta Qualia
Mio Babbino Caro
What You Never Know (Won't Hurt You)
Both Sides Now
The Mists of Islay
Laudate Dominum
She Moves Through the Fair

Treasure (UK and international edition, Decca, 2007)

This is my third international album for Decca. Dedicated to my Nanna, this album has a mixture of songs from her repertoire as a singer around Timaru, when she was much younger. It also marks my debut as a proper songwriter. I'm particularly proud of my 'hippie chick' track 'Let Me Lie', the mistitled 'Le Notte del Silenzio' and 'Melancholy Interlude', the tune that I discovered when I couldn't sleep in a hotel room after a concert in Japan.

Tracks
Let Me Lie
Le Notte del Silenzio (featuring Humphrey Berney)
Santa Lucia
Shenandoah
Whispering Hope
Summer Rain
Danny Boy
One Fine Day
The Heart Worships
E Pari Ra
Sonny
Summer Fly
Melancholy Interlude
Bist Du Bei Mir
Abide with Me

Celtic Treasure (USA, Canada, Australia and New Zealand edition, Decca, 2007)

Tracks
Let Me Lie
Scarborough Fair
Shenandoah
Summer Fly
Whispering Hope
Danny Boy
Summer Rain
The Last Rose of Summer
One Fine Day
Sonny
The Water Is Wide
Melancholy Interlude
Abide with Me

West Side Story (Universal Classics and Jazz, 2007)

Singing the role of Maria on this brand-new recording to mark the fiftieth anniversary of Leonard Bernstein's musical was a fantastic honour for me. Vittorio Grigolo sings Tony, the lead male role. The Royal Liverpool Philharmonic Orchestra is conducted by Nick Ingman.

Singles

Amazing Grace (released only in Japan, 2003)

Tracks
Amazing Grace
Beat of Your Heart
Benedictus
Amazing Grace (Instrumental)

Wiegenlied (released only in Japan, 2005)

Tracks
Wiegenlied (slow version)
Wiegenlied (fast version)
Wiegenlied (Japanese version)

Soundtracks

Nussknacker und Mausekönig (released 2004 in Germany)

Peaches and Creamy World

Mulan II (released 2005)

Here Beside Me

The Merchant of Venice (released 2005)

Bridal Ballad

Lilo and Stitch II (released 2006)

Always

The New World (released 2006)

Listen to the Wind

Guest appearances

I have the same management team as Aled Jones and the Choirboys and it was a real thrill for me to be able to sing on their albums. Aled is an old hand at making records and I made one of my first big appearances in front of the British critics and journalists when I sang with him at the Classical Brit Awards, so it was nice to be able to return the favour by appearing on his album. The Choirboys are a great group of young guys and I was really excited to be able to introduce them to my fans by singing on their debut release.

Singing 'Silent Night' with Aled Jones on *The Christmas Album* (UCJ, 2005)

Singing 'Do You Hear What I Hear?' with the Choirboys on *The Choirboys* (UCJ, 2005)

DVD

Hayley Westenra Live from New Zealand (Decca, 2005)

This DVD was recorded live at a specially staged concert at Wellington's St James Theatre in November 2004. It came after a long year of touring the world singing the songs from *Pure*. It was great to be able to come home to New Zealand and to perform them in front of the people who believed in me right from the start. The guests artists who appear on the DVD include the baritone Teddy Tahu Rhodes, my sister Sophie Westenra, the Musical Island Boys and the Wellington Cathedral Choir, accompanied by members of the Wellington Sinfonia. This concert was also broadcast as a special programme on the PBS network in the USA.

Songs
Pokarekare Ana
River of Dreams
In Trutina
Across the Universe of Time
May It Be
Beat of Your Heart
Aria
Who Painted the Moon Black?
How Many Stars?
Ave Maria
Down to the River
Amazing Grace
Benedictus
Mary Did You Know?
Both Sides Now
Never Say Goodbye
Wuthering Heights
Hine e Hine

Acknowledgements

I'm lucky to have been blessed with the most wonderful family on Earth. I would have achieved very little in my life without the love and support of my mum, Jill, and my dad, Gerald. As you have read, they have been with me every step of the way on my journey through life and on my journey through music. I couldn't have wished for two greater people to have had standing beside me. I love my sister Sophie and brother Isaac more than you can imagine. They are so patient and understanding about the demands that I've placed on their lives over the years. My Nanna,

Shirley Ireland, continues to be a huge inspiration to me in everything that I do. Basically, I couldn't survive without my family.

Good managers are hard to find and in Steve Abbott and Kathryn Nash at Bedlam Management I've found the best. Thank you both for your belief and hard work.

My record companies around the world have always given me an enormous amount of support and I'm proud to be part of the extended family of Decca Records, Universal Classics and Jazz UK and Universal Music around the globe. Particular thanks go to Bogdan Roscic, Peggy Schmidt, Fawzia Pirbhai, Judith Daniels, Mark Cavell and Jennifer Allen at Decca; to Dickon Stainer and Mark Wilkinson at UCJ; and to Adam Holt and Alister Cain in New Zealand.

Thank you to the whole team at Virgin Books who have patiently waited for me to complete this book, especially KT Forster, Carolyn Thorne and Gareth Fletcher.

Lastly, a massive thanks to Darren Henley. What a legend. It was such a pleasure writing this book with him. No one mentioned here is more deserving of the much-talked-about celebratory curry, to mark the end of working on this book.

Index